THE
WALKER
BOOK OF
CLASSIC
POETRY
AND
POETS

SELECTED BY
MICHAEL ROSEN

ILLUSTRATED BY
PAUL HOWARD

WALKER BOOKS
AND SUBSIDIARIES
LONDON • BOSTON • SYDNEY

For Harold
M.R.

For Amelia
P.H.

First published 1998 by Walker Books Ltd
87 Vauxhall Walk, London SE11 5HJ

This edition published 2001

10 9 8 7 6 5 4 3 2 1

Introduction, biographies and notes
© 1998 Michael Rosen
This selection of poems © as noted in
acknowledgements
Illustrations © 1998 Paul Howard

This book has been typeset in Columbus

Printed in Italy

British Library Cataloguing in
Publication Data:
a catalogue record for this book is
available from the British Library

ISBN 0-7445-8264-4

INTRODUCTION

THIS IS A BOOK OF CLASSIC POETRY, which is a way of saying that you will meet here poems that have lasted for many years, sometimes several hundreds of years. In that time they've remained popular; they've gone on mattering to people; many people have thought they said important things in a memorable way.

But it's quite easy to forget that poetry is made up by poets: real people who have parents, homes, different ways of earning a living, different ways of looking at the world around them. Each poet lived at a particular time in history and was affected by the events that took place at that particular time.

So in this book, where we know who wrote a poem, you'll find out something about the poet. A word of warning: what's said about them is only my view. If you read about that poet somewhere else you may well get a different view. One of the interesting things about poetry is that it's about ideas, and whenever you put ideas and people together, you get discussion and disagreement.

So in some ways this book is not only a book of classic poetry, it's also a book of classic poets. Often it gives you the chance to sample more than one poem by the same writer, helping you get a picture of what they were interested in, what mattered to them.

All the poets here wrote in English. Sometimes you will find collections that mix English-speaking poems with translations of poems from all over the world, and it is certainly true that poets over the centuries have talked to each other in different languages across national boundaries. (Shakespeare, for one, was very interested in how Italians wrote.)

But it's just as true that, under the umbrella of the word "English", many people from many different backgrounds and many different countries have been able to speak to each other in many different ways. In this book you will meet poets of British, American and Australian origins. And if you look more closely you will find interesting variations here – African-American, Irish, Scots, an Englishman born in India, an English woman with an Italian father, an American man with a Swedish father, and so on.

At the end of the book you'll find some notes. Information about poetry can sometimes be off-putting. What I've written is there only because I thought certain poems needed a few words of explanation to help you enjoy them more. Looking at how poetry works can also help you enjoy it. We need words like "internal combustion" and "diesel" to explain different kinds of engine, and we need words for different kinds of poetry. So at the back you'll also find some words that do just that: "ballad" and "lyric" and the like.

Finally, this book is also a book of pictures. The artist, Paul Howard, has read and re-read these poems. He's read pages and pages about the poets. He's even visited some of the places that the poets talk about. He has given us not only his vision of the poems, but portraits of the poets as well. This is all because he, like me, wants you to enjoy discovering some of the most brilliant imaginations of the English-speaking world.

Michael Rosen

CONTENTS

ELIZABETH BARRETT
BROWNING
1806-1861

~

"'For oh,' say the
children, 'we are
weary…'"
from *Child Labour*
❖ 40
The Ways of Love
❖ 41

HENRY
WADSWORTH
LONGFELLOW
1807-1882

~

The Slave's Dream
❖ 42
Paul Revere's Ride
❖ 46

EDGAR
ALLAN POE
1809-1849

~

The Bells ❖ 52
Eldorado ❖ 53

ALFRED, LORD
TENNYSON
1809-1892

~

Sweet and Low ❖ 54
The Eagle ❖ 55
Break, Break, Break
❖ 55
The Splendour Falls
❖ 56

EDWARD LEAR
1812-1888

~

Calico Pie ❖ 58
The Jumblies ❖ 60

ROBERT BROWNING
1812-1889

~

My Last Duchess
❖ 66

EMILY BRONTË
1818-1848

~

"High waving
heather, 'neath stormy
blasts bending"
❖ 70
"'Tis moonlight,
summer moonlight"
❖ 71

WALT WHITMAN
1819-1892

~

I Hear America
Singing ❖ 72
Mannahatta ❖ 74
Miracles ❖ 75
O Captain!
My Captain! ❖ 76

EMILY DICKINSON
1830-1886

~

"A Bird came down
the Walk –"
❖ 78
"A slash of Blue –"
❖ 80
"A word is dead"
❖ 80
"I'm Nobody!
Who are you?"
❖ 80
"The Wind begun
to knead the Grass –"
❖ 81

WILLIAM
SHAKESPEARE

1564-1616

William Shakespeare was born in Stratford-upon-Avon in England, the son of a business-man. As a young man, he went to London where he became an actor and writer in the theatre. One of his greatest achievements was to write speeches for the characters in his plays that are full of action, pictures, music, rhythm and, above all, feeling.

Jacques:

All the world's a stage,
And all the men and women merely players:
They have their exits and their entrances;
And one man in his time plays many parts,
His acts being seven ages. At first the infant,
Mewling and puking in the nurse's arms.
And then the whining school-boy, with his satchel
And shining morning face, creeping like snail
Unwillingly to school. And then the lover,
Sighing like furnace, with a woeful ballad
Made to his mistress' eyebrow. Then a soldier,
Full of strange oaths, and bearded like the pard,
Jealous in honour, sudden and quick in quarrel,
Seeking the bubble reputation
Even in the cannon's mouth. And then the justice,
In fair round belly with good capon lin'd,
With eyes severe, and beard of formal cut,
Full of wise saws and modern instances;
And so he plays his part. The sixth age shifts
Into the lean and slipper'd pantaloon,
With spectacles on nose and pouch on side,
His youthful hose, well sav'd, a world too wide
For his shrunk shank; and his big manly voice,
Turning again toward childish treble, pipes
And whistles in his sound. Last scene of all,
That ends this strange eventful history,
Is second childishness and mere oblivion,
Sans teeth, sans eyes, sans taste, sans everything. ◆

from *As You Like It*

THE SEVEN AGES OF MAN

All the world's a stage,
And all the men and
women merely players:
They have their exits
and their entrances;
And one man in his time
plays many parts...

Caliban:

Be not afeard; the isle is full of noises,
Sounds and sweet airs, that give delight and hurt not.
Sometimes a thousand twangling instruments
Will hum about mine ears, and sometime voices
That, if I then had waked after long sleep,
Will make me sleep again: and then, in dreaming,
The clouds methought would open and show riches
Ready to drop upon me, that, when I waked,
I cried to dream again. ◆

from *The Tempest*

Macbeth:

Tomorrow, and tomorrow, and tomorrow,
Creeps in this petty pace from day to day,
To the last syllable of recorded time;
And all our yesterdays have lighted fools
The way to dusty death. Out, out, brief candle,
Life's but a walking shadow, a poor player,
That struts and frets his hour upon the stage,
And then is heard no more: it is a tale
Told by an idiot, full of sound and fury,
Signifying nothing. ◆

from *Macbeth*

WILLIAM BLAKE

1757-1827
~

William Blake lived in London, where he struggled to support himself and his family by writing poetry, drawing and print-making. He illustrated his own poems and printed them himself. Blake was a rebel, whose writing attacked people in authority. He was also a visionary, someone whose mind is full of pictures or visions of the way the world is, or what it might become.

Nurse's Song

When the voices of children are heard on the green
And laughing is heard on the hill,
My heart is at rest within my breast
    And everything else is still.

"Then come home, my children, the sun is gone down
And the dews of night arise;
Come, come, leave off play, and let us away
Till the morning appears in the skies."

"No, no, let us play, for it is yet day
And we cannot go to sleep;
Besides, in the sky the little birds fly
And the hills are all cover'd with sheep."

"Well, well, go & play till the light fades away
And then go home to bed."
The little ones leaped & shouted & laugh'd
    And all the hills echoed. ◆

The Tyger

Tyger! Tyger! burning bright
In the forests of the night,
What immortal hand or eye
Could frame thy fearful symmetry?

In what distant deeps or skies
Burnt the fire of thine eyes?
On what wings dare he aspire?
What the hand dare seize the fire?

And what shoulder, and what art,
Could twist the sinews of thy heart?
And when thy heart began to beat,
What dread hand? And what dread feet?

What the hammer? What the chain?
In what furnace was thy brain?
What the anvil? What dread grasp
Dare its deadly terrors clasp?

When the stars threw down their spears,
And water'd heaven with their tears,
Did He smile His work to see?
Did He who made the Lamb make thee?

Tyger! Tyger! burning bright
In the forests of the night,
What immortal hand or eye,
Dare frame thy fearful symmetry? ◆

Tyger! Tyger! burning bright

"Skating"

WILLIAM
WORDSWORTH

1770-1850

William Wordsworth had a country childhood in the north-west of England, and this had a great effect on what he wrote. The other big influence on him was the time he spent in France during the French Revolution. So, many of Wordsworth's poems are about freedom, imagination and the wisdom of children and country people.

And in the frosty season, when the sun
Was set, and visible for many a mile
The cottage windows blazed through twilight gloom,
I heeded not their summons: happy time
It was indeed for all of us – for me
It was a time of rapture! Clear and loud
The village clock tolled six, – I wheeled about,
Proud and exulting like an untired horse
That cares not for his home. All shod with steel,
We hissed along the polished ice in games
Confederate, imitative of the chase
And woodland pleasures, – the resounding horn,
The pack loud chiming, and the hunted hare.
So through the darkness and the cold we flew,
And not a voice was idle; with the din
Smitten, the precipices rang aloud;
The leafless trees and every icy crag
Tinkled like iron; while far distant hills
Into the tumult sent an alien sound
Of melancholy not unnoticed, while the stars
Eastward were sparkling clear, and in the west
The orange sky of evening died away.
Not seldom from the uproar I retired

Into a silent bay, or sportively
Glanced sideway, leaving the tumultuous throng,
To cut across the reflex of a star
That fled, and, flying still before me, gleamed
Upon the glassy plain; and oftentimes,
When we had given our bodies to the wind,
And all the shadowy banks on either side
Came sweeping through the darkness, spinning still
The rapid line of motion, then at once
Have I, reclining back upon my heels,
Stopped short; yet still the solitary cliffs
Wheeled by me – even as if the earth had rolled
With visible motion her diurnal round!
Behind me did they stretch in solemn train,
Feebler and feebler, and I stood and watched
Till all was tranquil as a dreamless sleep. ◆

from *The Prelude*

Sonnet composed upon Westminster Bridge, 3rd September 1802

Earth has not anything to show more fair:
Dull would he be of soul who could pass by
A sight so touching in its majesty:
This City now doth, like a garment, wear
The beauty of the morning; silent, bare,
Ships, towers, domes, theatres, and temples lie
Open unto the fields, and to the sky;
All bright and glittering in the smokeless air.
Never did sun more beautifully steep
In his first splendour, valley, rock, or hill;
Ne'er saw I, never felt, a calm so deep!
The river glideth at his own sweet will:
Dear God! the very houses seem asleep;
And all that mighty heart is lying still! ◆

The Sun Has Long Been Set

The sun has long been set,
The stars are out by twos and threes,
The little birds are piping yet
Among the bushes and trees;
There's a cuckoo, and one or two thrushes,
And a far-off wind that rushes,
And a sound of water that gushes,
And the cuckoo's sovereign cry
Fills all the hollow of the sky.
Who would go parading
In London, and masquerading
On such a night of June
With that beautiful soft half-moon,
And all these innocent blisses?
On such a night as this is! ◆

SAMUEL
TAYLOR
COLERIDGE

1772-1834

*Coleridge was the
son of a vicar from
Devon, in England.
He was a friend of
William Wordsworth,
with whom he talked
about poetry,
imagination, language
and politics. Together
they wrote a book
called "Lyrical Ballads"
that helped to change
the sound and style of
poetry ever after.
Coleridge wrote about
emotions, dream-like
events and personal
feelings in strong
everyday language.*

Kubla Khan

In Xanadu did Kubla Khan
   A stately pleasure-dome decree:
Where Alph, the sacred river, ran
Through caverns measureless to man
   Down to a sunless sea.
So twice five miles of fertile ground
   With walls and towers were girdled round:
And there were gardens bright with sinuous rills
Where blossomed many an incense-bearing tree;
And here were forests ancient as the hills,
Enfolding sunny spots of greenery.

But O, that deep romantic chasm which slanted
Down the green hill athwart a cedarn cover!
A savage place! as holy and enchanted
As e'er beneath a waning moon was haunted
By woman wailing for her demon-lover!
And from this chasm, with ceaseless turmoil seething,
As if this earth in fast thick pants were breathing,
A mighty fountain momently was forced;
Amid whose swift half-intermitted burst
Huge fragments vaulted like rebounding hail,
Or chaffy grain beneath the thresher's flail:
And 'mid these dancing rocks at once and ever
It flung up momently the sacred river.
Five miles meandering with a mazy motion
Through wood and dale the sacred river ran,
Then reached the caverns measureless to man,
And sank in tumult to a lifeless ocean:
And 'mid this tumult Kubla heard from far
Ancestral voices prophesying war!

The shadow of the dome of pleasure
    Floated midway on the waves;
    Where was heard the mingled measure
    From the fountain and the caves.
It was a miracle of rare device,
A sunny pleasure-dome with caves of ice!

    A damsel with a dulcimer
    In a vision once I saw:
    It was an Abyssinian maid,
    And on her dulcimer she played,
    Singing of Mount Abora.
    Could I revive within me,
    Her symphony and song,
To such a deep delight 'twould win me,
That with music loud and long,
I would build that dome in air,
That sunny dome! those caves of ice!
And all who heard should see them there,
And all should cry, Beware! Beware!
His flashing eyes, his floating hair!
    Weave a circle round him thrice,
    And close your eyes with holy dread,
    For he on honey-dew hath fed,
    And drunk the milk of Paradise. ◆

The Destruction of Sennacherib

The Assyrian came down like the wolf on the fold,
And his cohorts were gleaming in purple and gold;
And the sheen of their spears was like stars on the sea,
When the blue wave rolls nightly on deep Galilee.

Like the leaves of the forest when Summer is green,
That host with their banners at sunset were seen;
Like the leaves of the forest when Autumn hath blown,
That host on the morrow lay wither'd and strown.

For the Angel of Death spread his wings on the blast,
And breathed in the face of the foe as he pass'd;
And the eyes of the sleepers waxed deadly and chill,
And their hearts but once heaved, and for ever grew still!

And there lay the steed with his nostril all wide,
But through it there roll'd not the breath of his pride;
And the foam of his gasping lay white on the turf,
And cold as the spray of the rock-beating surf.

And there lay the rider distorted and pale,
With the dew on his brow, and the rust on his mail;
And the tents were all silent, the banners alone,
The lances unlifted, the trumpet unblown.

And the widows of Ashur are loud in their wail,
And the idols are broke in the temple of Baal;
And the might of the Gentile, unsmote by the sword,
Hath melted like snow in the glance of the Lord! ◆

LORD BYRON

1788-1824
~

*George Gordon Byron,
who was born into a
not-very-well-off
English upper-class
family, lived in
Scotland until he was
ten. His adult life
was full of adventure,
drink, women and
brilliant poetry. As a
lord, he had the right
to speak in Parliament
where, to everyone's
surprise, he spoke up
for poor people.
His lifestyle caused a
scandal and he left
England when he was
twenty-eight. He died in
Greece, helping the
Greeks fight for freedom.*

That host on the morrow lay wither'd and strown

PERCY BYSSHE
SHELLEY

1792-1822

Shelley was born in Sussex, England. He could have become a member of Parliament like his father, but he was too rebellious for that. He was expelled from university for writing against religion, and in his poetry he attacked cruel rulers and hypocrites, and expressed his strong beliefs about love and his hopes for a better world. He died very young, drowning at sea off the coast of Italy.

Ozymandias

I met a traveller from an antique land
Who said: Two vast and trunkless legs of stone
Stand in the desert. Near them, on the sand,
Half sunk, a shattered visage lies, whose frown,
And wrinkled lip, and sneer of cold command,
Tell that its sculptor well those passions read
Which yet survive (stamped on these lifeless things),
The hand that mocked them and the heart that fed;
And on the pedestal these words appear:
"My name is Ozymandias, king of kings;
Look on my works, ye Mighty, and despair!"
Nothing beside remains. Round the decay
Of that colossal wreck, boundless and bare,
The lone and level sands stretch far away. ◆

Clock-a-clay

In the cowslip pips I lie,
Hidden from the buzzing fly,
While green grass beneath me lies,
Pearled wi' dew like fishes' eyes,
Here I lie, a clock-a-clay,
Waiting for the time of day.

While grassy forest quakes surprise,
And the wild wind sobs and sighs,
My gold home rocks as like to fall,
On its pillar green and tall:
When the pattering rain drives by
Clock-a-clay keeps warm and dry.

Day by day and night by night,
All the week I hide from sight;
In the cowslip pips I lie,
In rain and dew still warm and dry;
Day and night, and night and day,
Red, black-spotted clock-a-clay.

My home shakes in wind and showers,
Pale green pillar topped with flowers,
Bending at the wild wind's breath,
Till I touch the grass beneath;
Here I live, lone clock-a-clay,
Watching for the time of day. ◆

JOHN CLARE

1793-1864

John Clare was the son of a poor farm worker from Northamptonshire, England, and he worked on farms too. He collected local folk songs and his poems express a love for the countryside and an admiration of farm work. When he was forty-four, he became mentally ill and spent the rest of his life in hospitals where he went on writing moving poetry.

JOHN KEATS

1795–1821

Keats came from London where his father was a stable manager. He trained as an apothecary – someone who sells medicines – but decided at the age of twenty to become a poet instead. Although he was only twenty-six when he died, Keats wrote a huge number of poems. He conjured up a sense of longing and desire, often playing with images from a mysterious past. He died in Rome, Italy.

La Belle Dame Sans Merci

O what can ail thee, knight-at-arms,
    Alone and palely loitering?
The sedge has withered from the lake,
    And no birds sing.

O what can ail thee, knight-at-arms!
    So haggard, and so woe-begone?
The squirrel's granary is full,
    And the harvest's done.

I see a lily on thy brow
    With anguish moist and fever-dew,
And on thy cheek a fading rose
    Fast withereth too.

I met a lady in the meads,
    Full beautiful – a faery's child,
Her hair was long, her foot was light,
    And her eyes were wild.

I made a garland for her head,
    And bracelets too, and fragrant zone;
She looked at me as she did love,
    And made sweet moan.

I set her on my pacing steed
    And nothing else saw all day long,
For sidelong would she bend, and sing
    A faery's song.

She found me roots of relish sweet,
  And honey wild and manna-dew,
And sure in language strange she said,
  I love thee true.

She took me to her elfin grot,
  And there she wept and sighed full sore;
And there I shut her wild wild eyes
  With kisses four.

And there she lullèd me asleep,
  And there I dreamed – Ah! woe betide!
The latest dream I ever dreamed
  On the cold hill side.

I saw pale kings and princes too,
  Pale warriors, death-pale were they all:
They cried – "La belle Dame sans Merci
  Hath thee in thrall!"

I saw their starved lips in the gloam
  With horrid warning gapèd wide,
And I awoke and found me here
  On the cold hill side.

And this is why I sojourn here
  Alone and palely loitering,
Though the sedge is wither'd from the lake,
  And no birds sing. ◆

The Song of the Shirt

With fingers weary and worn,
With eyelids heavy and red,
A woman sat, in unwomanly rags,
Plying her needle and thread –
Stitch! stitch! stitch!
In poverty, hunger, and dirt,
And still with a voice of dolorous pitch
She sang the 'Song of the Shirt'.

"Work! work! work!
While the cock is crowing aloof!
And work – work – work,
Till the stars shine through the roof!
It's Oh! to be a slave
Along with the barbarous Turk,
Where woman has never a soul to save,
If this is Christian work!

"Work – work – work
Till the brain begins to swim:
Work – work – work
Till the eyes are heavy and dim!
Seam, and gusset, and band,
Band, and gusset, and seam,
Till over the buttons I fall asleep,
And sew them on in a dream!

THOMAS HOOD

1799-1845

Thomas Hood came from London where his father was a bookseller. In between working on magazines and journals, he wrote clever, witty and comic poetry. "The Song of the Shirt" was one of his few serious pieces. It appeared in Punch magazine in 1843 and became very popular, inspiring several artists to paint pictures to go with it.

"Oh, Men with Sisters dear!
 Oh, Men with Mothers and Wives!
 It is not linen you're wearing out,
 But human creatures' lives!
 Stitch – stitch – stitch,
 In poverty, hunger, and dirt,
 Sewing at once, with a double thread,
 A Shroud as well as a Shirt.

"But why do I talk of Death?
 That Phantom of grisly bone,
 I hardly fear its terrible shape,
 It seems so like my own –
 It seems so like my own,
 Because of the fasts I keep;
 Oh, God! that bread should be so dear,
 And flesh and blood so cheap!

"Work – work – work!
 My labour never flags;
 And what are its wages? A bed of straw,
 A crust of bread – and rags.
 That shatter'd roof – and this naked floor –
 A table – a broken chair –
 And a wall so blank, my shadow I thank
 For sometimes falling there!

"Work – work – work!
 From weary chime to chime,
Work – work – work –
 As prisoners work for crime!
Band, and gusset, and seam,
Seam, and gusset, and band,
 Till the heart is sick, and the brain benumb'd,
As well as the weary hand.

"Work – work – work,
 In the dull December light,
And work – work – work,
 When the weather is warm and bright –
While underneath the eaves
The brooding swallows cling
As if to show me their sunny backs
And twit me with the spring.

"Oh! but to breathe the breath
 Of the cowslip and primrose sweet –
With the sky above my head,
And the grass beneath my feet,
For only one short hour
To feel as I used to feel,
Before I knew the woes of want
And the walk that costs a meal!

"Oh! but for one short hour!
A respite however brief!
No blessed leisure for Love or Hope,
But only time for Grief!
A little weeping would ease my heart,
But in their briny bed
My tears must stop, for every drop
Hinders needle and thread!

"Seam, and gusset, and band,
Band, and gusset, and seam,
Work – work – work
Like the Engine that works by Steam!
A mere machine of iron and wood
That toils for Mammon's sake –
Without a brain to ponder and craze
Or a heart to feel – and break!"

With fingers weary and worn,
With eyelids heavy and red,
A woman sat in unwomanly rags,
Plying her needle and thread –
Stitch! stitch! stitch!
In poverty, hunger, and dirt,
And still with a voice of dolorous pitch, –
Would that its tone could reach the Rich! –
She sang this 'Song of the Shirt'! ◆

ELIZABETH
BARRETT
BROWNING

1806-1861

*Elizabeth Barrett,
the oldest of twelve
children, came from
a wealthy family who
lived in Herefordshire,
England. She suffered
from ill-health and
lived with her parents
until she was forty.
Then she met the poet
Robert Browning and
they married secretly
and ran away to Italy.
"The Ways of Love"
was written for
Browning, but it took
her three years to
pluck up the courage
to give it to him.*

"For oh," say the children, "we are weary
And we cannot run or leap;
If we cared for any meadows, it were merely
To drop down in them and sleep.
Our knees tremble sorely in the stooping,
We fall upon our faces, trying to go;
And underneath our heavy eyelids drooping
The reddest flower would look as pale as snow.
For, all day, we drag our burden tiring
Through the coal-dark, underground;
Or, all day, we drive the wheels of iron
In the factories, round and round.

"For all day the wheels are droning, turning;
Their wind comes in our faces,
Till our hearts turn, our heads with pulses burning,
And the walls turn in their places:
Turns the sky in the high window, blank and reeling,
Turns the long light that drops adown the wall,
Turn the black flies that crawl along the ceiling:
All are turning, all the day, and we with all.
And all day, the iron wheels are droning,
And sometimes we could pray,
'O ye wheels' (breaking out in a mad moaning)
'Stop! be silent for to-day!'" ◆

from *Child Labour*

40

The Ways of Love

How do I love thee? Let me count the ways.
    I love thee to the depth and breadth and height
    My soul can reach, when feeling out of sight
For the ends of being and ideal grace.
I love thee to the level of every day's
    Most quiet need, by sun and candlelight.
    I love thee freely, as men strive for right;
I love thee purely, as they turn from praise.
I love thee with the passion put to use
    In my old griefs, and with my childhood's faith.
I love thee with a love I seemed to lose
    With my lost saints, – I love thee with the breath,
Smiles, tears, of all my life! – and, if God choose,
    I shall but love thee better after death. ◆

HENRY
WADSWORTH
LONGFELLOW

1807-1882

*Longfellow was born
in Maine, USA, and
as quite a young man
became professor at
America's most famous
university, Harvard,
where he stayed for the
rest of his life. He
became one of the most
popular poets of his
day throughout the
English-speaking world
and was the author of
the best-known modern
epic poem, "Hiawatha".*

The Slave's Dream

Beside the ungathered rice he lay,
His sickle in his hand;
His breast was bare, his matted hair
Was buried in the sand.
Again, in the mist and shadow of sleep,
He saw his Native Land.

Wide through the landscape of his dreams
The lordly Niger flowed;
Beneath the palm-trees on the plain
Once more a king he strode;
And heard the tinkling caravans
Descend the mountain road.

He saw once more his dark-eyed queen
Among her children stand;
They clasped his neck, they kissed his cheeks,
They held him by the hand! –
A tear burst from the sleeper's lids
And fell into the sand.

And then at furious speed he rode
Along the Niger's bank:
His bridle-reins were golden chains,
And, with a martial clank,
At each leap he could feel his scabbard of steel
Smiting his stallion's flank.

Before him, like a blood-red flag,
The bright flamingoes flew;
From morn till night he followed their flight,
O'er plains where the tamarind grew,
Till he saw the roofs of Caffre huts,
And the ocean rose to view.

At night he heard the lion roar,
And the hyena scream,
And the river-horse, as he crushed the reeds
Beside some hidden stream;
And it passed, like a glorious roll of drums
Through the triumph of his dream.

The forests, with their myriad tongues,
Shouted of liberty;
And the Blast of the Desert cried aloud,
With a voice so wild and free,
That he started in his sleep and smiled
At their tempestuous glee.

He did not feel the driver's whip,
Nor the burning heat of day;
For Death had illumined the land of Sleep,
And his lifeless body lay
A worn-out fetter, that the soul
Had broken and thrown away! ◆

Beside the ungathered rice he lay

Paul Revere's Ride

Listen, my children, and you shall hear
Of the midnight ride of Paul Revere,
On the eighteenth of April, in Seventy-five;
Hardly a man is now alive
Who remembers that famous day and year.

He said to his friend, "If the British march
By land or sea from the town tonight,
Hang a lantern aloft in the belfry arch
Of the North Church tower as a signal light –
One, if by land, and two, if by sea;
And I on the opposite shore will be,
Ready to ride and spread the alarm
Through every Middlesex village and farm,
For the country folk to be up and to arm."

Then he said, "Good night!" and with muffled oar
Silently rowed to the Charlestown shore,
Just as the moon rose over the bay,
Where swinging wide at her moorings lay

The Somerset, British man-of-war;
A phantom ship, with each mast and spar
Across the moon like a prison bar,
And a huge black hulk, that was magnified
By its own reflection in the tide.

Meanwhile, his friend, through alley and street,
Wanders and watches with eager ears,
Till in the silence around him he hears
The muster of men at the barrack door,
The sound of arms, and the tramp of feet,
And the measured tread of the grenadiers,
Marching down to their boats on the shore.

Then he climbed the tower of the Old North Church,
By the wooden stairs, with stealthy tread,
To the belfry-chamber overhead,
And startled the pigeons from their perch
On the sombre rafters, that round him made
Masses and moving shapes of shade –
By the trembling ladder, steep and tall,
To the highest window in the wall,
Where he paused to listen and look down
A moment on the roofs of the town,
And the moonlight flowing over all.

Beneath, in the churchyard, lay the dead,
In their night-encampment on the hill,
Wrapped in silence so deep and still
That he could hear, like a sentinel's tread,
The watchful night-wind, as it went
Creeping along from tent to tent,
And seeming to whisper, "All is well!"
A moment only he feels the spell
Of the place and the hour, and the secret dread
Of the lonely belfry and the dead;
For suddenly all his thoughts are bent
On a shadowy something far away,
Where the river widens to meet the bay –
A line of black that bends and floats
On the rising tide, like a bridge of boats.

Meanwhile, impatient to mount and ride,
Booted and spurred, with a heavy stride
On the opposite shore walked Paul Revere.
Now he patted his horse's side,
Now gazed at the landscape far and near,
Then, impetuous, stamped the earth,
And turned and tightened his saddle-girth;
But mostly he watched with eager search
The belfry-tower of the Old North Church,
As it rose above the graves on the hill,
Lonely and spectral and sombre and still.

And lo! as he looks, on the belfry's height
A glimmer, and then a gleam of light!
He springs to the saddle, the bridle he turns,
But lingers and gazes, till full on his sight
A second lamp in the belfry burns!

A hurry of hoofs in a village street,
A shape in the moonlight, a bulk in the dark,
And beneath, from the pebbles, in passing, a spark
Struck out by a steed flying fearless and fleet;
That was all! And yet, through the gloom and the light
The fate of a nation was riding that night;
And the spark struck out by that steed in his flight,
Kindled the land into flame with its heat.

He has left the village and mounted the steep,
And beneath him, tranquil and broad and deep,
Is the Mystic, meeting the ocean tides;
And under the alders, that skirt its edge,
Now soft on the sand, now loud on the ledge,
Is heard the tramp of his steed as he rides.

It was twelve by the village clock,
When he crossed the bridge into Medford town.
He heard the crowing of the cock,
And the barking of the farmer's dog,
And felt the damp of the river fog,
That rises after the sun goes down.

It was one by the village clock,
When he galloped into Lexington.
He saw the gilded weathercock
Swim in the moonlight as he passed,
And the meeting-house windows, blank and bare,
Gaze at him with a spectral glare,
As if they already stood aghast
At the bloody work they would look upon.

It was two by the village clock,
When he came to the bridge in Concord town.
He heard the bleating of the flock,
And the twitter of birds among the trees,
And felt the breath of the morning breeze
Blowing over the meadows brown.

And one was safe and asleep in his bed
Who at the bridge would be first to fall,
Who that day would be lying dead,
Pierced by a British musket-ball.

You know the rest. In the books you have read,
How the British Regulars fired and fled –
How the farmers gave them ball for ball,
From behind each fence and farmyard wall,
Chasing the redcoats down the lane,
Then crossing the fields to emerge again
Under the trees at the turn of the road,
And only pausing to fire and load.

So through the night rode Paul Revere;
And so through the night went his cry of alarm
To every Middlesex village and farm –
A cry of defiance, and not of fear,
A voice in the darkness, a knock at the door,
And a word that shall echo for evermore!
For, borne on the night-wind of the past,
Through all our history, to the last,
In the hour of darkness and peril and need,
The people will waken and listen to hear
The hurrying hoofbeats of that steed,
And the midnight message of Paul Revere. ◆

EDGAR
ALLAN POE

1809-1849

Poe was born in
Massachusetts, USA,
the son of travelling
actors. He became an
orphan and was looked
after by a tobacco
merchant. He tried
university and the army
but neither worked out.
He then married his
very young cousin and
struggled to support
his household by
writing stories,
newspaper articles and
poems. He is one of
the world's most famous
writers of horror,
mystery and fantasy
stories and poems.

The Bells

Hear the sledges with the bells –
    Silver bells!
What a world of merriment their melody foretells!
    How they tinkle, tinkle, tinkle,
    In the icy air of night!
    While the stars that oversprinkle
    All the heavens, seem to twinkle
    With a crystalline delight;
    Keeping time, time, time,
    In a sort of Runic rhyme,
To the tintinnabulation that so musically wells
    From the bells, bells, bells, bells,
        Bells, bells, bells –
From the jingling and the tinkling of the bells. ◆

Eldorado

Gaily bedight,
A gallant knight,
In sunshine and in shadow,
Had journeyed long,
Singing a song,
In search of Eldorado.

But he grew old –
This knight so bold –
And o'er his heart a shadow
Fell as he found
No spot of ground
That looked like Eldorado.

And, as his strength
Failed him at length,
He met a pilgrim shadow:
"Shadow," said he,
"Where can it be,
This land of Eldorado?"

"Over the mountains
Of the Moon,
Down the valley of the Shadow,
Ride, boldly ride,"
The shade replied,
"If you seek for Eldorado." ◆

ALFRED, LORD
TENNYSON

1809-1892

*Tennyson was the
son of a churchman
from Lincolnshire,
England. Later in life,
he and his family lived
on the Isle of Wight.
He began publishing
poetry when he was
only eighteen, and in
time he became the
best-known poet in
Victorian England.
Some of his poetry is
the most musical verse
ever written in English.*

Sweet and Low

Sweet and low, sweet and low,
    Wind of the western sea,
Low, low, breathe and blow,
    Wind of the western sea!
Over the rolling waters go,
Come from the dying moon, and blow,
    Blow him again to me;
While my little one, while my pretty one, sleeps.

Sleep and rest, sleep and rest,
    Father will come to thee soon;
Rest, rest, on mother's breast,
    Father will come to thee soon;
Father will come to his babe in the nest,
Silver sails all out of the west
    Under the silver moon:
Sleep my little one, sleep, my pretty one, sleep. ◆

The Eagle

He clasps the crag with crooked hands;
Close to the sun in lonely lands,
Ring'd with the azure world, he stands.
The wrinkled sea beneath him crawls;
He watches from his mountain walls,
And like a thunderbolt he falls. ◆

Break, Break, Break

Break, break, break
    On thy cold grey stones, O Sea!
And I would that my tongue could utter
    The thoughts that arise in me.

O well for the fisherman's boy,
    That he shouts with his sister at play!
O well for the sailor lad,
    That he sings in his boat on the bay!

And the stately ships go on
    To their haven under the hill;
But O for the touch of a vanish'd hand
    And the sound of a voice that is still!

Break, break, break,
    At the foot of thy crags, O Sea!
But the tender grace of a day that is dead
    Will never come back to me. ◆

The Splendour Falls

The splendour falls on castle walls
And snowy summits old in story:
The long light shakes across the lakes,
And the wild cataract leaps in glory.
Blow, bugle, blow, set the wild echoes flying,
Blow, bugle; answer, echoes, dying, dying, dying.

O hark, O hear! how thin and clear,
And thinner, clearer, farther going!
O sweet and far from cliff and scar
The horns of Elfland faintly blowing!
Blow, let us hear the purple glens replying:
Blow, bugle; answer, echoes, dying, dying, dying.

O love, they die in yon rich sky,
They faint on hill or field or river:
Our echoes roll from soul to soul,
And grow for ever and for ever.
Blow, bugle, blow, set the wild echoes flying,
And answer, echoes, answer, dying, dying, dying. ◆

EDWARD
LEAR

1812-1888

~

*Lear was born in
London, the twentieth
child of a businessman.
He was brought up
mainly by his older
sister, Ann, and earned
a living doing drawings
of animals and plants.
He was later able to
become a full time
poet because the Earl
of Derby gave him
money. He travelled all
over the world writing
and drawing, but
suffered from illness
and depression. Behind
the fun in his poems,
you can often sense
loneliness.*

Calico Pie

I

Calico Pie,
　The little Birds fly,
Down to the calico tree,
　Their wings were blue,
　And they sang "Tilly-loo!"
　Till away they flew, –
And they never came back to me!
They never came back!
They never came back!
　They never came back to me!

II

Calico Jam,
　The little Fish swam,
Over the syllabub sea,
　He took off his hat,
　To the Sole and the Sprat,
　And the Willeby-wat, –
But he never came back to me!
He never came back!
He never came back!
　He never came back to me!

III

    Calico Ban,
    The little Mice ran,
To be ready in time for tea,
    Flippity flup,
    They drank it all up,
    And danced in the cup, –
But they never came back to me!
They never came back!
They never came back!
    They never came back to me!

IV

    Calico Drum,
    The Grasshoppers come,
    The Butterfly, Beetle, and Bee,
    Over the ground,
    Around and round,
    With a hop and a bound, –
But they never came back!
They never came back!
They never came back!
    They never came back to me! ◆

The Jumblies

I

They went to sea in a Sieve, they did,
   In a Sieve they went to sea:
In spite of all their friends could say,
On a winter's morn, on a stormy day,
   In a Sieve they went to sea!
And when the Sieve turned round and round,
And every one cried, "You'll all be drowned!"
They called aloud, "Our Sieve ain't big,
But we don't care a button! We don't care a fig!
   In a Sieve we'll go to sea!"
Far and few, far and few,
Are the lands where the Jumblies live;
Their heads are green, and their hands are blue,
And they went to sea in a Sieve.

II

They sailed away in a Sieve, they did,
    In a Sieve they sailed so fast,
With only a beautiful pea-green veil
Tied with a riband by way of a sail,
    To a small tobacco-pipe mast;
And every one said, who saw them go,
"O won't they be soon upset, you know!
For the sky is dark, and the voyage is long,
And happen what may, it's extremely wrong
    In a Sieve to sail so fast!"
Far and few, far and few,
Are the lands where the Jumblies live;
Their heads are green, and their hands are blue,
And they went to sea in a Sieve.

III

The water it soon came in, it did,
    The water it soon came in;
So to keep them dry, they wrapped their feet
In a pinky paper all folded neat,
    And they fastened it down with a pin.
And they passed the night in a crockery-jar,
And each of them said, "How wise we are!
Though the sky be dark, and the voyage be long,
Yet we never can think we were rash or wrong,
    While round in our Sieve we spin!"
Far and few, far and few,
Are the lands where the Jumblies live;
Their heads are green, and their hands are blue,
And they went to sea in a Sieve.

IV

And all night long they sailed away;
 And when the sun went down,
They whistled and warbled a moony song
To the echoing sound of a coppery gong,
 In the shade of the mountains brown.
"O Timballo! How happy we are,
 When we live in a sieve and a crockery-jar,
And all night long in the moonlight pale,
We sail away with a pea-green sail,
 In the shade of the mountains brown!"
Far and few, far and few,
Are the lands where the Jumblies live;
Their heads are green, and their hands are blue,
And they went to sea in a Sieve.

V

They sailed to the Western Sea, they did,
    To a land all covered with trees,
And they bought an Owl, and a useful Cart,
And a pound of Rice, and a Cranberry Tart,
    And a hive of silvery Bees.
And they bought a Pig, and some green Jack-daws,
And a lovely Monkey with lollipop paws,
And forty bottles of Ring-Bo-Ree,
    And no end of Stilton Cheese.
Far and few, far and few,
Are the lands where the Jumblies live;
Their heads are green, and their hands are blue,
And they went to sea in a Sieve.

VI

And in twenty years they all came back,
  In twenty years or more,
And every one said, "How tall they've grown!
For they've been to the Lakes, and the Torrible Zone,
  And the hills of the Chankly Bore;"
And they drank their health, and gave them a feast
Of dumplings made of beautiful yeast;
And every one said, "If we only live,
We too will go to sea in a Sieve, –
  To the hills of the Chankly Bore!"
Far and few, far and few,
Are the lands where the Jumblies live;
Their heads are green, and their hands are blue,
And they went to sea in a Sieve. ◆

Robert
Browning

1812-1889

~

Browning, the son of
a clerk in the Bank of
England, was brought
up by his sister in
London. He tried uni-
versity but gave it up
and concentrated on
writing plays and
poems. He travelled in
Russia and lived with
his wife, Elizabeth
Barrett Browning, in
Italy until she died.
Though he was not
hugely popular in his
day, many people now
see that he was one
of the most inventive
poets of his time.

My Last Duchess

Ferrara

That's my last Duchess painted on the wall,
Looking as if she were alive. I call
That piece a wonder, now: Fra Pandolf's hands
Worked busily a day, and there she stands.
Will't please you sit and look at her? I said
"Fra Pandolf" by design, for never read
Strangers like you that pictured countenance,
The depth and passion of its earnest glance,
But to myself they turned (since none puts by
The curtain I have drawn for you, but I)
And seemed as they would ask me, if they durst,
How such a glance came there; so, not the first
Are you to turn and ask thus. Sir, 'twas not
Her husband's presence only, called that spot
Of joy into the Duchess' cheek: perhaps
Fra Pandolf chanced to say "Her mantle laps
Over my lady's wrist too much," or "Paint
Must never hope to reproduce the faint
Half-flush that dies along her throat": such stuff
Was courtesy, she thought, and cause enough
For calling up that spot of joy. She had
A heart – how shall I say? – too soon made glad,
Too easily impressed; she liked whate'er
She looked on, and her looks went everywhere.
Sir, 'twas all one! My favour at her breast,

The dropping of the daylight in the West,
The bough of cherries some officious fool
Broke in the orchard for her, the white mule
She rode with round the terrace – all and each
Would draw from her alike the approving speech,
Or blush, at least. She thanked men – good! but thanked
Somehow – I know not how – as if she ranked
My gift of a nine-hundred-years-old name
With anybody's gift. Who'd stoop to blame
This sort of trifling? Even had you skill
In speech – (which I have not) – to make your will
Quite clear to such an one, and say, "Just this
Or that in you disgusts me; here you miss,
Or there exceed the mark" – and if she let
Herself be lessoned so, nor plainly set
Her wits to yours, forsooth, and made excuse,
 – E'en then would be some stooping; and I choose
Never to stoop. Oh sir, she smiled, no doubt,
Whene'er I passed her; but who passed without
Much the same smile? This grew; I gave commands;
Then all smiles stopped together. There she stands
As if alive. Will't please you rise? We'll meet
The company below, then. I repeat,
The Count your master's known munificence
Is ample warrant that no just pretence
Of mine for dowry will be disallowed;
Though his fair daughter's self, as I avowed
At starting, is my object. Nay, we'll go
Together down, sir. Notice Neptune, though,
Taming a sea-horse, thought a rarity,
Which Claus of Innsbruck cast in bronze for me! ◆

That's my last Duchess painted on the wall

EMILY
BRONTË

1818-1848
〜

A long with her sisters
Charlotte and Anne,
Emily was brought up
in their father's
vicarage in Yorkshire,
England. All three
women were writers,
Emily's most famous
work being the novel
"Wuthering Heights".
In her lifetime Emily
was overshadowed by
her sisters, but over the
years she has come to
be seen as one of the
most original poets
of the century —
profound, passionate
and mysterious.

High waving heather, 'neath stormy blasts bending,
Midnight and moonlight and bright shining stars;
Darkness and glory rejoicingly blending,
Earth rising to heaven and heaven descending,
Man's spirit away from its drear dungeon sending,
Bursting the fetters and breaking the bars.

All down the mountain sides, wild forests lending
One mighty voice to the life-giving wind;
Rivers their banks in the jubilee rending,
Fast through the valleys a reckless course wending,
Wider and deeper their waters extending,
Leaving a desolate desert behind.

Shining and lowering and swelling and dying,
Changing for ever from midnight to noon;
Roaring like thunder, like soft music sighing,
Shadows on shadows advancing and flying,
Lightning-bright flashes the deep gloom defying,
Coming as swiftly and fading as soon. ◆

'Tis moonlight, summer moonlight,
All soft and still and fair;
The solemn hour of midnight
Breathes sweet thoughts everywhere,

But most where trees are sending
Their breezy boughs on high,
Or stooping low are lending
A shelter from the sky.

And there in those wild bowers
A lovely form is laid;
Green grass and dew-steeped flowers
Wave gently round her head. ◆

WALT
WHITMAN

1819-1892

Walt Whitman came from New York, where he worked as an office boy. Later he turned his hand to printing, teaching, journalism and politics. His first book, "Leaves of Grass", contained twelve poems that were meant to free American writing from what Whitman saw as "stifling" old Europe. He invented a new kind of poetry, full of great personal and political feeling, made up of the vigorous rhythms of everyday speech and the Bible.

I Hear America Singing

I hear America singing, the varied carols I hear,
Those of mechanics, each one singing his
as it should be blithe and strong,
The carpenter singing his
as he measures
his plank or beam,

The mason singing his
as he makes ready for work,
or leaves off work,
The boatman singing what
belongs to him in his boat,
the deckhand singing on the steamboat deck,
The shoemaker singing as he sits
on his bench, the hatter
singing as he stands,

72

The wood-cutter's song,
   the ploughboy's on his way in the morning,
      or at noon intermission or at sundown,
         The delicious singing of the mother,
            or of the young wife at work,
               or of the girl sewing or washing,

Each singing what belongs to him
   or her and to none else,
The day what belongs to the day —
   at night the party of young fellows, robust, friendly,
Singing with open mouths their strong melodious songs. ◆

Mannahatta

I was asking for something specific and perfect for my city,
Whereupon lo! upsprang the aboriginal name.
Now I see what there is in a name, a word, liquid, sane,
    unruly, musical, self-sufficient,
I see that the word of my city is that word from of old,
Because I see that word nested in nests of water-bays, superb,
Rich, hemm'd thick all around with sailships and
    steamships, an island sixteen miles long, solid-founded.
Numberless crowded streets, high growths of iron, slender,
    strong, light, splendidly uprising toward clear skies,
Tides swift and ample, well-loved by me, toward sundown,
The flowing sea-currents, the little islands, larger
    adjoining islands, the heights, the villas,
The countless masts, the white shore-steamers, the lighters,
    the ferry-boats, the black sea-steamers, well-model'd,
The down-town streets, the jobbers' houses of business,
    the houses of business of the ship-merchants and
    money-brokers, the river-streets,
Immigrants arriving, fifteen or twenty thousand in a week,
The carts hauling goods, the manly race of drivers of
    horses, the brown-faced sailors,
The summer air, the bright sun shining, and the sailing clouds aloft,
The winter snows, the sleigh-bells, the broken ice in the river,
    passing along up or down with the flood-tide or ebb-tide,
The mechanics of the city, the masters, well-form'd,
    beautiful-faced, looking you straight in the eyes,
Trottoirs throng'd, vehicles, Broadway, the women, the shops and shows,
A million people – manners free and superb – open voices –
    hospitality – the most courageous and friendly young men,
City of hurried and sparkling waters! city of spires and masts!
City nested in bays! my city! ◆

Miracles

Why, who makes much of a miracle?
As to me I know of nothing else but miracles,
Whether I walk the streets of Manhattan,
Or dart my sight over the roofs of houses toward the sky,
Or wade with naked feet along the beach just
    in the edge of the water,
Or stand under trees in the woods,
Or talk by day with anyone I love, or sleep in the bed
    at night with anyone I love,
Or sit at table at dinner with the rest,
Or look at strangers opposite me riding in the car,
Or watch honey-bees busy around the hive
    of a summer fore-noon,
Or animals feeding in the fields,
Or birds, or the wonderfulness of insects in the air,
Or the wonderfulness of the sundown, or of stars shining
    so quiet and bright,
Or the exquisite delicate thin curve of the
    new moon in spring;
These with the rest, one and all, are to me miracles,
The whole referring, yet each distinct and in its place.
To me every hour of the light and dark is a miracle,
Every cubic inch of space is a miracle,
Every square yard of the surface of the earth
    is spread with the same,
Every foot of the interior swarms with the same.
To me the sea is a continual miracle,
The fishes that swim – the rocks – the motion of the waves –
    the ships with men in them,
What stranger miracles are there? ◆

O Captain! My Captain!

O Captain! my Captain! our fearful trip is done,
The ship has weather'd every rack, the prize we sought is won,
The port is near, the bells I hear, the people all exulting,
While follow eyes the steady keel, the vessel grim and daring;
   But O heart! heart! heart!
    O the bleeding drops of red,
     Where on the deck my Captain lies,
      Fallen cold and dead.

O Captain! my Captain! rise up and hear the bells;
Rise up – for you the flag is flung – for you the bugle trills,
For you bouquets and ribbon'd wreaths – for you the shores a-crowding,
For you they call, the swaying mass, their eager faces turning;
   Here Captain! dear father!
    This arm beneath your head!
     It is some dream that on the deck,
      You've fallen cold and dead.

My Captain does not answer, his lips are pale and still,
My father does not feel my arm, he has no pulse nor will,
The ship is anchor'd safe and sound, its voyage closed and done,
From fearful trip the victor ship comes in with object won;
   Exult O shores, and ring O bells!
    But I with mournful tread,
     Walk the deck my Captain lies,
      Fallen cold and dead. ◆

EMILY
DICKINSON

1830–1886

*Emily Dickinson was
born in Massachusetts,
USA. She was the
daughter of a lawyer
and had an academic
education. In her early
twenties she was a
lively, sociable woman
but slowly she retreated
into her home, never
going out, never
meeting people. Right
from childhood she
wrote poems but only
seven were seen in print
in her lifetime. When
she died, over two
thousand amazing,
intense, dazzling poems
were found.*

A Bird came down the Walk –
He did not know I saw –
He bit an Angleworm in halves
And ate the fellow, raw,

And then he drank a Dew
From a convenient Grass –
And then hopped sidewise to the Wall
To let a Beetle pass –

He glanced with rapid eyes
That hurried all around –
They looked like frightened Beads, I thought –
He stirred his Velvet Head

Like one in danger, Cautious,
I offered him a Crumb
And he unrolled his feathers
And rowed him softer home –

Than Oars divide the Ocean,
Too silver for a seam –
Or Butterflies, off Banks of Noon
Leap, plashless as they swim. ◆

A slash of Blue –
A sweep of Gray –
Some scarlet patches on the way,
Compose an Evening Sky –
A little purple – slipped between –
Some Ruby Trousers hurried on –
A Wave of Gold –
A Bank of Day –
This just makes out the Morning Sky. ◆

A word is dead
When it is said,
Some say.
I say it just
Begins to live
That day. ◆

I'm Nobody! Who are you?
Are you – Nobody – too?
Then there's a pair of us!
Don't tell! they'll banish us – you know!
How dreary – to be – Somebody!
How public – like a Frog –
To tell your name – the livelong June –
To an admiring Bog! ◆

The Wind begun to knead the Grass –
As Women do a Dough –
He flung a Hand full at the Plain –
A Hand full at the Sky –
The Leaves unhooked themselves from Trees –
And started all abroad –
The Dust did scoop itself like Hands –
And throw away the Road –
The Wagons quickened on the Street –
The Thunders gossiped low –
The Lightning showed a Yellow Head –
And then a livid Toe –
The Birds put up the Bars to Nests –
The Cattle flung to Barns –
Then came one drop of Giant Rain –
And then, as if the Hands
That held the Dams – had parted hold –
The Waters Wrecked the Sky –
But overlooked my Father's House –
Just Quartering a Tree – ◆

CHRISTINA
ROSSETTI

1830-1894

*Christina Rossetti's
father was an Italian
living in London and
she was brought up in
an atmosphere full of
literature, religion and
politics. She was often
ill, and spent a lot of
time at home writing
poetry. Some of her
poems were religious,
some specially for
children and some
romantic. Her work
is full of a beautiful
sense of sadness and
yearning, and quite
often death is not far
away.*

Who has seen the wind?
Neither I nor you:
But when the leaves hang trembling
The wind is passing thro'.

Who has seen the wind?
Neither you nor I:
But when the trees bow down their heads
The wind is passing by. ◆

Sonnet

Remember me when I am gone away,
　　Gone far away into the silent land;
　　When you can no more hold me by the hand,
Nor I half turn to go yet turning stay.
Remember me when no more day by day
　　You tell me of our future that you planned:
　　Only remember me; you understand
It will be late to counsel then or pray.
Yet if you should forget me for a while
　　And afterwards remember, do not grieve:
　　For if the darkness and corruption leave
　　A vestige of the thoughts that once I had,
Better by far that you should forget and smile
　　Than that you should remember and be sad. ◆

LEWIS
CARROLL

1832-1898
~

Lewis Carroll's real name was Charles Lutwidge Dodgson. He was the son of a vicar and lived in various places in Cheshire and Yorkshire. He spent most of his adult life attached to a college at Oxford University. It was there that he wrote his famous books about Alice, and though he wrote other poems, it is the ones in the Alice books that are the best-known and probably the funniest.

The Mock Turtle's Song

"Will you walk a little faster?"
   said a whiting to a snail.
"There's a porpoise close behind us,
   and he's treading on my tail.
See how eagerly the lobsters and
   the turtles all advance!
They are waiting on the shingle –
   will you come and join the dance?
Will you, won't you, will you, won't you,
   will you join the dance?
Will you, won't you, will you, won't you,
   won't you join the dance?

"You can really have no notion how
    delightful it will be,
When they take us up and throw us,
    with the lobsters, out to sea!"
But the snail replied "Too far, too far!"
    and gave a look askance –
Said he thanked the whiting kindly,
    but he would not join the dance.
Would not, could not, would not,
    could not, would not join the dance.
Would not, could not, would not,
    could not, could not join the dance.

"What matters it how far we go?"
    his scaly friend replied.
"There is another shore, you know,
    upon the other side.
The further off from England
    the nearer is to France –
Then turn not pale, beloved snail,
    but come and join the dance?
Will you, won't you, will you,
    won't you, won't you join the dance?
Will you, won't you, will you,
    won't you, won't you join the dance?" ◆

from *Alice's Adventures in Wonderland*

How doth the little crocodile
    Improve his shining tail,
And pour the waters of the Nile
    On every golden scale!

How cheerfully he seems to grin,
    How neatly spreads his claws,
And welcomes little fishes in
    With gently smiling jaws! ◆

from *Alice's Adventures in Wonderland*

Jabberwocky

'Twas brillig, and the slithy toves
    Did gyre and gimble in the wabe;
All mimsy were the borogroves,
    And the mome raths outgrabe.

"Beware the Jabberwock, my son!
    The jaws that bite, the claws that catch!
Beware the Jubjub bird, and shun
    The frumious Bandersnatch!"

He took his vorpal sword in hand:
    Long time the manxome foe he sought –
So rested he by the Tumtum tree,
    And stood a while in thought.

And as in uffish thought he stood,
    The Jabberwock, with eyes of flame,
Came whiffling through the tulgey wood,
    And burbled as it came!

One, two! One, two! And through and through
    The vorpal blade went snicker-snack!
He left it dead, and with its head
    He went galumphing back.

"And hast thou slain the Jabberwock?
    Come to my arms, my beamish boy!
O frabjous day! Callooh! Callay!"
    He chortled in his joy.

'Twas brillig, and the slithy toves
    Did gyre and gimble in the wabe;
All mimsy were the borogroves,
    And the mome raths outgrabe. ◆

from *Alice's Adventures in Wonderland*

Iroquois Prayer

We return thanks to our mother, the earth,
   which sustains us.
We return thanks to the rivers and streams,
   which supply us with water.
We return thanks to all herbs, which furnish
   medicines for the cure of our diseases.
We return thanks to the corn, and to her sisters,
   the beans and squashes, which give us life.
We return thanks to the bushes and trees,
   which provide us with fruit.
We return thanks to the wind, which,
   moving the air, has banished diseases.
We return thanks to the moon and stars,
   which have given to us their light
   when the sun was gone.
We return thanks to our grandfather Hé-no,
   that he has protected his grandchildren from
   witches and reptiles, and has given to us his rain.
We return thanks to the sun, that he has looked upon
   the earth with a beneficent eye.
Lastly, we return thanks to the Great Spirit,
   in whom is embodied all goodness, and who
   directs all things for the good of his children. ◆

Anonymous

90

Swing Low, Sweet Chariot

I ain't never been to heaven but I been told,
Comin' for to carry me home,
That the streets in heaven are paved with gold,
Comin' for to carry me home.

Swing low, sweet chariot,
Comin' for to carry me home,
Swing low, sweet chariot,
Comin' for to carry me home.

That ain't all, I got more besides –
I been to the river an' I been baptize'.

Lemme tell you what's a matter o' fact,
If you ever leave the devil, you never go back.

You see them sisters dress so fine?
Well, they ain't got Jesus on their mind.

If salvation was a thing money could buy,
Then the rich would live an' the poor would die.

But I'm so glad God fix it so,
That the rich must die just as well as the poor! ◆

Anonymous

THOMAS
HARDY

1840-1928
~

*Hardy grew up in
Dorset, England. He
wrote poetry all his life
but at first it was his
novels that people
loved. He gave up writ-
ing the novels, though,
when he became sad-
dened and annoyed by
the way the public
reacted to his
last two, "Jude the
Obscure" and "Tess of
the d'Urbervilles".
For the last thirty-three
years of his life he
turned almost entirely
to writing poetry, full
of memories and
sights taken from his
earlier life.*

Snow in the Suburbs

Every branch big with it,
Bent every twig with it;
Every fork like a white web-foot;
Every street and pavement mute:
Some flakes have lost their way, and grope back upward, when
Meeting those meandering down they turn and descend again.
The palings are glued together like a wall,
And there is no waft of wind with the fleecy fall.

A sparrow enters the tree,
Whereon immediately
A snow-lump thrice his own slight size
Descends on him and showers his head and eyes,
And overturns him,
And near inurns him,
And lights on a nether twig, when its brush
Starts off a volley of other lodging lumps with a rush.

The steps are a blanched slope,
Up which, with feeble hope,
A black cat comes, wide-eyed and thin;
And we take him in. ◆

Throwing a Tree

The two executioners stalk along over the knolls,
Bearing two axes with heavy heads shining and wide,
And a long limp two-handled saw toothed for cutting great boles,
And so they approach the proud tree that bears the death-mark on its side.

Jackets doffed they swing axes and chop away just above ground,
And the chips fly about and lie white on the moss and fallen leaves;
Till a broad deep gash in the bark is hewn all the way round,
And one of them tries to hook upward a rope, which at last he achieves.

The saw then begins, till the top of the tall giant shivers:
The shivers are seen to grow greater each cut than before:
They edge out the saw, tug the rope; but the tree only quivers,
And kneeling and sawing again, they step back to try pulling once more.

Then, lastly, the living mast sways, further sways: with a shout
Job and Ike rush aside. Reached the end of its long staying powers
The tree crashes downward: it shakes all its neighbours throughout,
And two hundred years' steady growth has been ended in less than two hours. ◆

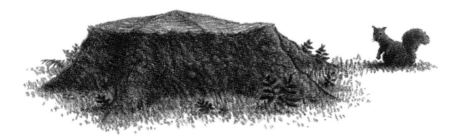

At the Railway Station, Upway

"There is not much that I can do,
  For I've no money that's quite my own!"
Spoke up the pitying child –
A little boy with a violin
At the station before the train came in, –
"But I can play my fiddle to you,
  And a nice one 'tis, and good in tone!"

The man in the handcuffs smiled;
The constable looked, and he smiled, too,
  As the fiddle began to twang;
And the man in the handcuffs suddenly sang
  With grimful glee:
"This life so free
  Is the thing for me!"
And the constable smiled, and said no word,
As if unconscious of what he heard;
And so they went on till the train came in –
The convict, and the boy with the violin. ◆

ROBERT LOUIS
STEVENSON

1850-1894
~

Stevenson grew up in Edinburgh, Scotland. He turned away from what his parents wanted him to be, a lawyer, and took up writing instead. He wrote plays, novels, children's stories like "Treasure Island", and poetry for both adults and children. "A Child's Garden of Verses" is the first book of poetry for children which is entirely about the poet's own childhood written from the child's point of view.

A Good Play

We built a ship upon the stairs
All made of the back-bedroom chairs,
And filled it full of sofa pillows
To go a-sailing on the billows.

We took a saw and several nails,
And water in the nursery pails;
And Tom said, "Let us also take
An apple and a slice of cake;"—
Which was enough for Tom and me
To go a-sailing on, till tea.

We sailed along for days and days,
And had the very best of plays;
But Tom fell out and hurt his knee,
So there was no one left but me. ◆

Block City

What are you able to build with your blocks?
Castles and palaces, temples and docks.
Rain may keep raining, and others go roam,
But I can be happy and building at home.

Let the sofa be mountains, the carpet be sea,
There I'll establish a city for me:
A kirk and a mill and a palace beside,
And a harbour as well where my vessels may ride.

Great is the palace with pillar and wall,
A sort of a tower on top of it all,
And steps coming down in an orderly way
To where my toy vessels lie safe in the bay.

This one is sailing and that one is moored:
Hark to the song of the sailors on board!
And see on the steps of my palace, the kings
Coming and going with presents and things!

Now that I have done with it, down let it go!
All in a moment the town is laid low.
Block upon block lying scattered and free,
What is there left of my town by the sea?

Yet as I saw it, I see it again,
The kirk and the palace, the ships and the men,
And as long as I live and where'er I may be,
I'll always remember my town by the sea. ◆

From a Railway Carriage

Faster than fairies, faster than witches,
Bridges and houses, hedges and ditches;
And charging along like troops in a battle,
All through the meadows the horses and cattle:
All of the sights of the hill and the plain
Fly as thick as driving rain;
And ever again, in the wink of an eye,
Painted stations whistle by.

Here is a child who clambers and scrambles,
All by himself and gathering brambles;
Here is a tramp who stands and gazes;
And there is the green for stringing the daisies!

Here is a cart run away in the road
Lumping along with man and load;
And here is a mill and there is a river:
Each a glimpse and gone for ever! ◆

Where Go the Boats

Dark brown is the river,
    Golden is the sand.
It flows along for ever,
    With trees on either hand.

Green leaves a-floating,
    Castles of the foam,
Boats of mine a-boating –
    Where will all come home?

On goes the river
    And out past the mill,
Away down the valley,
    Away down the hill.

Away down the river,
    A hundred miles or more,
Other little children
    Shall bring my boats ashore. ◆

On goes the river

ELLA WHEELER
WILCOX

1850-1919

*Ella Wheeler Wilcox
was born in Wisconsin,
USA, and caused
a sensation when she
brought out books of
poems full of passionate
and romantic feeling.
She soon became one
of the most popular
writers in America and
beyond. She also wrote
short stories, novels
and an autobiography.
Her work seems
simple but it is full of
well-expressed truth.*

Solitude

Laugh, and the world laughs with you,
Weep, and you weep alone;
For the sad old earth must borrow its mirth,
But has trouble enough of its own.
Sing, and the hills will answer,
Sigh, it is lost on the air;
The echoes bound to a joyful sound,
But shrink from voicing care.

Rejoice, and men will seek you,
Grieve, and they turn and go;
They want full measure of all your pleasure,
But they do not need your woe.
Be glad, and your friends are many,
Be sad, and you lose them all;
There are none to decline your nectared wine,
But alone you must drink life's gall.

Feast, and your halls are crowded,
Fast, and the world goes by.
Succeed and give, and it helps you live,
But no man can help you die;
For there is room in the halls of pleasure
For a long and lordly train,
But one by one we must all file on
Through the narrow aisles of pain. ◆

BANJO
PATERSON

1864-1941

*Andrew Barton
Paterson, usually
known as "Banjo"
Paterson, was born in
New South Wales,
Australia. He worked as
a lawyer and journalist
but he is most famous
for "Waltzing
Matilda", a folk song
that he rewrote. He
wrote many ballads
about rural Australian
life that are funny with
strong popular appeal.*

Waltzing Matilda

Once a jolly swagman camped by a billabong,
    Under the shade of a coolibah-tree,
And he sang as he watched and waited till his billy boiled,
"Who'll come a-waltzing Matilda with me?"

    Waltzing Matilda,
        Waltzing Matilda,

    Who'll come a-waltzing Matilda with me?"
And he sang as he watched and waited till his billy boiled,
"Who'll come a-waltzing Matilda with me?"

Down came a jumbuck to drink at the billabong:
    Up jumped the swagman and grabbed him with glee.
And he sang as he shoved that jumbuck in his tucker-bag,
"You'll come a-waltzing Matilda with me.

    Waltzing Matilda,
        Waltzing Matilda,

    You'll come a-waltzing Matilda with me."
And he sang as he shoved that jumbuck in his tucker-bag,
"You'll come a-waltzing Matilda with me."

Up rode a squatter, mounted on his thoroughbred;
Down came the troopers, one, two, three:
"Who's that jolly jumbuck you've got in your tucker-bag?
You'll come a-waltzing Matilda with me.

Waltzing Matilda,
Waltzing Matilda,

You'll come a-waltzing Matilda with me.
Who's that jolly jumbuck you've got in your tucker-bag?
You'll come a-waltzing Matilda with me."

Up jumped the swagman and sprang into the billabong;
"You'll never catch me alive!" said he;
And his ghost may be heard as you pass by that billabong,
"You'll come a-waltzing Matilda with me!

Waltzing Matilda,
Waltzing Matilda,

You'll come a-waltzing Matilda with me!"
And his ghost may be heard as you pass by that billabong,
"You'll come a-waltzing Matilda with me!" ◆

Mulga Bill's Bicycle

'Twas Mulga Bill, from Eaglehawk, that caught the cycling craze;
He turned away the good old horse that served him many days;
He dressed himself in cycling clothes, resplendent to be seen;
He hurried off to town and bought a shining new machine;
And as he wheeled it through the door, with air of lordly pride,
The grinning shop assistant said, "Excuse me, can you ride?"
"See here, young man," said Mulga Bill, "from Walgett to the sea,
From Conroy's Gap to Castlereagh, there's none can ride like me.
I'm good all round at everything, as everybody knows,
Although I'm not the one to talk – I hate a man that blows.
But riding is my special gift, my chiefest, sole delight;
Just ask a wild duck can it swim, a wild cat can it fight.
There's nothing clothed in hair or hide, or built of flesh or steel,
There's nothing walks or jumps, or runs, on axle, hoof, or wheel,
But what I'll sit, while hide will hold and girths and straps are tight;
I'll ride this here two-wheeled concern right straight away at sight."

'Twas Mulga Bill, from Eaglehawk, that sought his own abode,
That perched above the Dead Man's Creek, beside the mountain road.
He turned the cycle down the hill and mounted for the fray,
But ere he'd gone a dozen yards it bolted clean away.
It left the track, and through the trees, just like a silver streak,
It whistled down the awful slope towards the Dead Man's Creek.

It shaved a stump by half an inch, it dodged a big white-box:
The very wallaroos in fright went scrambling up the rocks,
The wombats hiding in their caves dug deeper underground,
But Mulga Bill, as white as chalk, sat tight to every bound.
It struck a stone and gave a spring that cleared a fallen tree,
It raced beside a precipice as close as close could be;
And then, as Mulga Bill let out one last despairing shriek,
It made a leap of twenty feet into the Dead Man's Creek.

'Twas Mulga Bill, from Eaglehawk, that slowly swam ashore:
He said, "I've had some narrer shaves and lively rides before;
I've rode a wild bull round a yard to win a five-pound bet,
But this was sure the derndest ride that I've encountered yet.
I'll give that two-wheeled outlaw best; it's shaken all my nerve
To feel it whistle through the air and plunge and buck and swerve.
It's safe at rest in Dead Man's Creek – we'll leave it lying still;
A horse's back is good enough henceforth for Mulga Bill." ◆

RUDYARD
KIPLING

1865-1936

Kipling was born in Bombay, India, but went to school in England. He went back to India for a while as a journalist, and all his life he wrote newspaper articles, novels, short stories, children's books like "The Jungle Book", and poetry. In his poetry he was often able to capture the sound of different kinds of people talking, and his writing was always immensely popular.

A Smuggler's Song

If you wake at midnight and hear a horse's feet,
Don't go drawing back the blind, or looking in the street,
Them that asks no questions isn't told a lie.
Watch the wall, my darling, while the Gentlemen go by!
Five and twenty ponies,
Trotting through the dark –
Brandy for the Parson,
'Baccy for the Clerk;
Laces for a lady; letters for a spy,
And watch the wall, my darling, while the Gentlemen go by!

Running round the woodlump if you chance to find
Little barrels, roped and tarred, all full of brandy-wine,
Don't you shout to come and look, nor use 'em for your play.
Put the brushwood back again – and they'll be gone next day!

If you see the stable-door setting open wide;
If you see a tired horse lying down inside;
If your mother mends a coat cut about and tore;
If the lining's wet and warm – don't you ask no more!

If you meet King George's men, dressed in blue and red,
You be careful what you say, and mindful what is said.
If they call you "pretty maid", and chuck you 'neath the chin,
Don't you tell where no one is, nor yet where no one's been!

Knocks and footsteps round the house – whistles after dark –
You've no call for running out till the housedogs bark.
Trusty's here and Pincher's here, and see how dumb they lie –
They don't fret to follow when the Gentlemen go by!

If you do as you've been told, 'likely there's a chance,
You'll be give a dainty doll, all the way from France,
With a cap of Valenciennes, and a velvet hood –
A present from the Gentlemen, along o' being good!
        Five and twenty ponies,
        Trotting through the dark –
        Brandy for the Parson,
        'Baccy for the Clerk.
Them that asks no questions isn't told a lie –
Watch the wall, my darling, while the Gentlemen go by! ◆

The Deep-sea Cables

The wrecks dissolve above us;
their dust drops down from afar –
Down to the dark, to the utter dark,
where the blind white sea-snakes are.
There is no sound, no echo of sound,
in the deserts of the deep,
Or the great grey level plains of ooze
where the shell-burred cables creep.

Here in the womb of the world – here on the tie-ribs of earth
Words, and the words of men, flicker and flutter and beat –
Warning, sorrow, and gain, salutation and mirth –
For a Power troubles the Still that has neither voice nor feet.

They have wakened the timeless Things;
they have killed their father Time;
Joining hands in the gloom,
a league from the last of the sun.
Hush! Men talk to-day o'er the waste of the ultimate slime,
And a new Word runs between: whispering, "Let us be one!" ◆

The Way Through the Woods

They shut the road through the woods
Seventy years ago.
Weather and rain have undone it again,
And now you would never know
There was once a road through the woods
Before they planted the trees.
It is underneath the coppice and heath
And the thin anemones.
Only the keeper sees
That, where the ring-dove broods,
And the badgers roll at ease,
There was once a road through the woods.

Yet, if you enter the woods
Of a summer evening late,
When the night-air cools on the trout-ringed pools
Where the otter whistles his mate,
(They fear not men in the woods,
Because they see so few.)
You will hear the beat of a horse's feet,
And the swish of a skirt in the dew,
Steadily cantering through
The misty solitudes,
As though they perfectly knew
The old lost road through the woods …
But there is no road through the woods. ◆

WILLIAM
BUTLER YEATS

1865-1939

Yeats was born in Dublin, Ireland, the son of a painter. He went to school in London and for a while he wanted to be a painter too. But at twenty-one he turned to writing and editing. He collected and retold Irish legends and fairytales and wrote a great deal of beautiful and lyrical poetry. All his life he was interested in Irish politics and eventually he became a senator. In 1923 he received the world's top award for writing, the Nobel Prize for Literature.

The Song of Wandering Aengus

I went out to the hazel wood,
Because a fire was in my head,
And cut and peeled a hazel wand,
And hooked a berry to a thread;
And when white moths were on the wing,
And moth-like stars were flickering out,
I dropped the berry in a stream
And caught a little silver trout.

When I laid it on the floor
I went to blow the fire aflame,
But something rustled on the floor,
And some one called me by my name:
It had become a glimmering girl
With apple blossom in her hair
Who called me by my name and ran
And faded through the brightening air.

Though I am old with wandering
Through hollow lands and hilly lands,
I will find out where she has gone,
And kiss her lips and take her hands;
And walk among long dappled grass,
And pluck till time and times are done
The silver apples of the moon,
The golden apples of the sun. ◆

An Irish Airman
Foresees His Death

I know that I shall meet my fate
Somewhere among the clouds above;
Those that I fight I do not hate,
Those that I guard I do not love;
My country is Kiltartan Cross,
My countrymen Kiltartan's poor,
No likely end could bring them loss
Or leave them happier than before.
Nor law, nor duty bade me fight,
Nor public men, nor cheering crowds,
A lonely impulse of delight
Drove to this tumult in the clouds;
I balanced all, brought all to mind,
The years to come seemed waste of breath,
A waste of breath the years behind
In balance with this life, this death. ◆

He Wishes for the Cloths of Heaven

Had I the heavens' embroidered cloths,
Enwrought with golden and silver light,
The blue and the dim and the dark cloths
Of night and light and the half-light,
I would spread the cloths under your feet:
But I, being poor, have only my dreams;
I have spread my dreams under your feet;
Tread softly because you tread on my dreams. ◆

The Lake Isle of Innisfree

I will arise and go now, and go to Innisfree,
And a small cabin build there, of clay and wattles made:
Nine bean-rows will I have there, a hive for the honey-bee,
And live alone in the bee-loud glade.

And I shall have some peace there, for peace comes dropping slow,
Dropping from the veils of the morning to where the cricket
sings;
There midnight's all a glimmer, and noon a purple glow,
And evening full of the linnet's wings.

I will arise and go now, for always night and day
I hear lake water lapping with low sounds by the shore;
While I stand on the roadway, or on the pavements grey,
I hear it in the deep heart's core. ◆

HENRY
LAWSON

1867-1922

*Henry Lawson was
born in New South
Wales, Australia, the
son of a Norwegian
sailor. At the age of
nine he suffered a severe
loss of hearing which
made learning very
difficult for him —
despite being one of the
brightest in his class.
As an adult, he lived
for many years in the
Australian outback
where he wrote hun-
dreds of humorous sto-
ries and story-poems
about farm-life, called
"bush ballads".*

Reedy River

Ten miles down Reedy River
   A pool of water lies,
And all the year it mirrors
   The changes in the skies.
Within that pool's broad bosom
   Is room for all the stars;
Its bed of sand has drifted
   O'er countless rocky bars.

Around the lower edges
   There waves a bed of reeds,
Where water-rats are hidden
   And where the wild-duck breeds;
And grassy slopes rise gently
   To ridges long and low,
Where the groves of wattle flourish
   And native bluebells grow.

Beneath the granite ridges
   The eye may just discern
Where Rocky Creek emerges
   From deep green banks of fern;
And standing tall between them,
   The drooping she-oaks cool
The hard, blue-tinted waters
   Before they reach the pool.

Ten miles down Reedy River
    One Sunday afternoon,
I rode with Mary Campbell
    To that broad, bright lagoon;
We left our horses grazing
    Till shadows climbed the peak,
And strolled beneath the she-oaks
    On the banks of Rocky Creek.

Then home along the river
    That night we rode a race,
And the moonlight lent a glory
    To Mary Campbell's face;
I pleaded for my future
    All through that moonlight ride,
Until our weary horses
    Drew closer side by side.

Ten miles from Ryan's Crossing
    And five below the peak,
I built a little homestead
    On the banks of Rocky Creek;
I cleared the land and fenced it
    And ploughed the rich red loam;
And my first crop was golden
    When I brought Mary home.

Now still down Reedy River
    The grassy she-oaks sigh;
The waterholes still mirror
    The pictures in the sky;
The golden sand is drifting
    Across the rocky bars;
And over all for ever
    Go sun and moon and stars.

But of the hut I builded
    There are no traces now,
And many rains have levelled
    The furrows of my plough.
The glad bright days have vanished;
    For sombre branches wave
Their wattle-blossom golden
    Above my Mary's grave. ◆

HILAIRE
BELLOC

1870-1953
≈

*Belloc was born in
France but went to
school and university
in England. For a while
he was a Member of
Parliament, and all his
life he wrote articles
about travel, religion,
politics and literature.
He wrote novels and
travel books but his
first and most popular
publication was his
poetry for children.
His favourite way of
writing, whether it was
for adults or children,
was to mock and tease.*

Tarantella

Do you remember an Inn,
Miranda?
Do you remember an Inn?
And the tedding and the spreading
Of the straw for a bedding,
And the fleas that tease in the High Pyrenees,
And the wine that tasted of the tar,
And the cheers and the jeers of the young muleteers
(Under the dark of the vine verandah)?
Do you remember an Inn,
Miranda?
Do you remember an Inn?
And the cheers and the jeers of the young muleteers
Who hadn't got a penny,
And who weren't paying any,
And the hammer at the doors and the Din?

And the Hip! Hop! Hap!
Of the clap
Of the hands to the twirl and the swirl
Of the girl gone chancing,
Glancing,
Dancing,
Backing and advancing,
Snapping of the clapper to the spin
Out and in —

And the Ting, Tong, Tang of the Guitar!
Do you remember an Inn,
Miranda?
Do you remember an Inn?
Never more,
Miranda,
Never more.
Only the high peaks hoar:
And Aragon a torrent at the door.
No sound
In the walls of the Halls where falls
The tread
Of the feet of the dead to the ground.
No sound:
Only the boom
Of the far Waterfall like Doom. ◆

Silver

Slowly, silently, now the moon
Walks the night in her silver shoon;
This way, and that, she peers, and sees
Silver fruit upon silver trees;
One by one the casements catch
Her beams beneath the silvery thatch;
Couched in his kennel, like a log,
With paws of silver sleeps the dog;
From their shadowy cote the white breasts peep
Of doves in a silver-feathered sleep;
A harvest mouse goes scampering by,
With silver claws, and silver eye;
And moveless fish in the water gleam,
By silver reeds in a silver stream. ◆

The Listeners

"Is there anybody there?" said the Traveller,
Knocking on the moonlit door;
And his horse in the silence champed the grasses
Of the forest's ferny floor:
And a bird flew up out of the turret,
Above the Traveller's head:
And he smote upon the door again a second time;
"Is there anybody there?" he said.

WALTER
DE LA MARE

1873-1956

De la Mare was born in Kent, England, and began work as a clerk in an oil company where he stayed for eighteen years. But all that time, and later, he worked away at writing short stories and poetry for adults and children, including the classic children's poetry book, "Peacock Pie". He also edited some very popular poetry anthologies, which reflect his great interest in fantasy, dreams, mystery and childhood.

But no one descended to the Traveller;
No head from the leaf-fringed sill
Leaned over and looked into his grey eyes,
Where he stood perplexed and still.
But only a host of phantom listeners
That dwelt in the lone house then
Stood listening in the quiet of the moonlight
To that voice from the world of men:
Stood thronging the faint moonbeams on the dark stair,
That goes down to the empty hall,
Hearkening in an air stirred and shaken
By the lonely Traveller's call.
And he felt in his heart their strangeness,
Their stillness answering his cry,
While his horse moved, cropping the dark turf,
'Neath the starred and leafy sky;
For he suddenly smote on the door, even
Louder, and lifted his head:
"Tell them I came, and no one answered,
That I kept my word," he said.
Never the least stir made the listeners,
Though every word he spake
Fell echoing through the shadowiness of the still house
From the one man left awake:
Ay, they heard his foot upon the stirrup,
And the sound of iron on stone,
And how the silence surged softly backward,
When the plunging hoofs were gone. ◆

Five Eyes

In Hans' old Mill his three black cats
Watch his bins for the thieving rats.
Whisker and claw, they crouch in the night,
Their five eyes smouldering green and bright:
Squeaks from the flour sacks, squeaks from where
The cold wind stirs on the empty stair,
Squeaking and scampering, everywhere.
Then down they pounce, now in, now out,
At whisking tail, and sniffing snout;
While lean old Hans he snores away
Till peep of light at break of day;
Then up he climbs to his creaking mill,
Out come his cats all grey with meal –
Jekkel, and Jessup, and one-eyed Jill. ◆

The Road Not Taken

Two roads diverged in a yellow wood,
And sorry I could not travel both
And be one traveller, long I stood
And looked down one as far as I could
To where it bent in the undergrowth;

Then took the other, as just as fair,
And having perhaps the better claim,
Because it was grassy and wanted wear;
Though as for that the passing there
Had worn them really about the same,

And both that morning equally lay
In leaves no step had trodden black.
Oh, I kept the first for another day!
Yet knowing how way leads on to way,
I doubted if I should ever come back.

I shall be telling this with a sigh
Somewhere ages and ages hence:
Two roads diverged in a wood, and I —
I took the one less travelled by,
And that has made all the difference. ◆

ROBERT FROST

1874-1963

One of the most surprising things about Frost is that he was born in San Francisco, because he is best-known for writing about life on the other side of America. For a while he lived in England but spent the last forty-eight years of his life in New Hampshire, USA. In this time, his poetry became hugely popular, with its observation of country life mingled with his wise and thoughtful views.

Stopping by Woods on a Snowy Evening

Whose woods these are I think I know.
His house is in the village though;
He will not see me stopping here
To watch his woods fill up with snow.

My little horse must think it queer
To stop without a farmhouse near
Between the woods and frozen lake
The darkest evening of the year.

He gives his harness bells a shake
To ask if there is some mistake.
The only other sound's the sweep
Of easy wind and downy flake.

The woods are lovely, dark and deep.
But I have promises to keep,
And miles to go before I sleep,
And miles to go before I sleep. ◆

The Pasture

I'm going out to clean the pasture spring;
I'll only stop to rake the leaves away
(And wait to watch the water clear, I may):
I shan't be gone long. — You come too.

I'm going out to fetch the little calf
That's standing by the mother. It's so young,
It totters when she licks it with her tongue.
I shan't be gone long. — You come too. ◆

Adlestrop

Yes. I remember Adlestrop –
The name, because one afternoon
Of heat the express-train drew up there
Unwontedly. It was late June.

The steam hissed. Some one cleared his throat.
No one left and no one came
On the bare platform. What I saw
Was Adlestrop – only the name

And willows, willow-herb, and grass,
And meadowsweet, and haycocks dry,
No whit less still and lonely fair
Than the high cloudlets in the sky.

And for that minute a blackbird sang
Close by, and round him, mistier,
Farther and farther, all the birds
Of Oxfordshire and Gloucestershire. ◆

EDWARD
THOMAS

1878-1917

Edward Thomas was born and brought up in London before going to university. He made a living from writing, but not from his poems. Thomas was killed in the First World War, and his quiet nature poetry was published after that. He was an admirer and friend of Robert Frost.

What I saw was Adlestrop — only the name

CARL
SANDBURG

1878-1967
~

*Sandburg came from
a Swedish background
but he lived his life in
and around Chicago,
USA. His poetry
was amongst the first
to give voice to
American speech and
he developed a way
of writing that sounds
like people chatting or
telling you something.
His poetry is often
hard-hitting, attacking
war, cruelty and greed.
At other times with its
jazzy style, it praises
city life.*

Arithmetic

Arithmetic is where numbers fly
    like pigeons in and out of your head.

Arithmetic tells you how many you lose
    or win if you know how many
    you had before you lost or won.

Arithmetic is numbers seven eleven
    all good children go to heaven –
    or five six bundle of sticks.

Arithmetic is numbers you squeeze from
    your head to your hand to your pencil
    to your paper till you get the answer.

Arithmetic is where the answer is right
    and everything is nice and you can look
    out of the window and see the blue sky –
    or the answer is wrong and
    you have to start all over and try again and
    see how it comes out this time.

If you take a number and double it and
    double it again and then double it a few more
    times, the number gets bigger and bigger and
    goes higher and higher and only arithmetic
    can tell you what the number is when you
    decide to quit doubling.

Arithmetic is where you have to multiply –
  and you carry the multiplication table
  in your head and hope you won't lose it.

If you have two animal crackers, one good and one bad,
  and you eat one and a striped zebra
  with streaks all over him eats the other,
  how many animal crackers will you have
  if somebody offers you five six seven and
  you say No no no and you say Nay nay nay and
  you say Nix nix nix?

If you ask your mother for one fried egg for breakfast
  and she gives you two fried eggs and
  you eat both of them, who is better in arithmetic,
  you or your mother? ◆

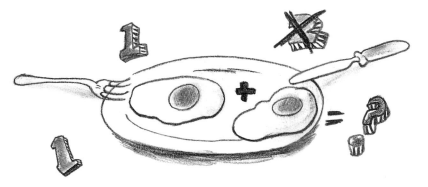

SKYSCRAPER

By day the
skyscraper looms in the
smoke and sun and has a soul.
Prairie and valley, streets of
the city, pour people into it
and they mingle among its
twenty floors and are poured
out again back to the streets,
prairies and valleys.

It is the men and women,
boys and girls so poured
in and out all day that
give the building a soul
of dreams and thoughts
and memories.
(Dumped in the sea or
fixed in a desert, who
would care for the build-
ing or speak its name or
ask a policeman the way
to it?)
Elevators slide on their
cables and tubes catch
letters and parcels and
iron pipes carry gas and
water in and sewage out.
Wires climb with secrets,
carry light and carry
words, and tell terrors and
profits and loves — curses
of men grappling plans of
business and questions of
women in plots of love.

138

IN

OUT

Hour by hour
the caissons reach
down to the rock of
the earth and hold the
building to a turning planet.
Hour by hour the girders
play as ribs and reach out and
hold together the stone walls
and floors.

Hour by hour the hand of
the mason and the stuff of
the mortar clinch the pieces
and parts to the shape an
architect voted.

Hour by hour the sun and
the rain, the air and the rust,
and the press of time
running into centuries, play
on the building inside and
out and use it.

Men who sunk the pilings
and mixed the mortar are
laid in graves where the
wind whistles a wild song
without words

And so are men who strung
the wires and fixed the pipes
and tubes and those who
saw it rise floor by floor.

Souls of them all are
here, even the hod
carrier begging at
back doors hundreds
of miles away and
the bricklayer who
went to state's prison
for shooting another
man while drunk.
(One man fell from a
girder and broke his
neck at the end of a
straight plunge – he
is here – his soul has
gone into the stones
of the building.)

On the office doors from tier to tier – hundreds of names and each name standing for a face written across with a dead child, a passionate lover, a driving ambition for a million dollar business or a lobster's ease of life.

Behind the signs on the doors they work and the walls tell nothing from room to room.

Ten-dollar-a-week stenographers take letters from corporation officers, lawyers, efficiency engineers, and tons of letters go bundled from the building to all ends of the earth.

Smiles and tears of each officegirl go into the soul of the building just the same as the master-men who rule the building.

Hands of clocks turn to noon hours and each floor empties its men and women who go away and eat and come back to work.

Toward the end of the afternoon all work slackens and all jobs go slower as the people feel day closing on them.

One by one the floors are emptied… The uniformed elevator men are gone. Pails clang… Scrubbers work, talking in foreign tongues.

Broom and water and mop clean from the floors human dust and spit, and machine grime of the day.

Spelled in electric fire on the roof are words telling miles of houses and people where to buy a thing for money. The sign speaks till midnight.

Darkness on the hallways. Voices echo. Silence holds... Watchmen walk slow from floor to floor and try the doors. Revolvers bulge from their hip pockets... Steel safes stand in corners. Money is stacked in them.

A young watchman leans at a window and sees the lights of barges butting their way across a harbor, nets of red and white lanterns in a railroad yard, and a span of glooms splashed with lines of white and blurs of crosses and clusters over the sleeping city.

By night the skyscraper looms in the smoke and the stars and has a soul. ◆

JOHN
MASEFIELD

1878-1967

*Masefield came
from Herefordshire,
England. His mother
died when he was six
and he was brought up
by relatives. He trained
to be a merchant
seaman but deserted,
became a tramp and
turned eventually to
writing. Some of
Masefield's most famous
poems, including
"Cargoes", were amongst
the earliest things he
wrote. Later he turned
to writing novels,
including some for
children, like "The Box
of Delights".*

Cargoes

Quinquireme of Nineveh from distant Ophir
Rowing home to haven in sunny Palestine,
With a cargo of ivory
And apes and peacocks,
Sandalwood, cedarwood, and sweet white wine.

Stately Spanish galleon coming from the Isthmus,
Dipping through the tropics by the palm-grove shores,
With a cargo of diamonds,
Emeralds, amethysts,
Topazes, and cinnamon, and gold moidores.

Dirty British coaster with a salt-caked smoke-stack,
Butting through the Channel in the mad March days,
With a cargo of Tyne coal,
Road-rails, pig-lead,
Firewood, ironware, and cheap tin trays. ◆

The General

"Good morning; good morning!" the General said
When we met him last week on our way to the line.
Now the soldiers he smiled at are most of 'em dead,
And we're cursing his staff for incompetent swine.
"He's a cheery old card," grunted Harry to Jack
As they slogged up to Arras with rifle and pack.

But he did for them both by his plan of attack. ◆

SIEGFRIED
SASSOON

1886-1967
〜

Sassoon almost seemed to have lived three different lives — before, during and after the First World War. He came from a wealthy, leisured back-ground in Kent and Sussex, England, before arriving in the terrible and ghastly conditions of that war. Here his writing changed from being rural and quiet to savage, bitter attacks on what was happening around him. Then, when it was over, he returned to his old style.

143

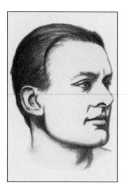

T. S. ELIOT

1888-1965

*Eliot was born in
Missouri, USA, but
settled in England in
his twenties. For a while
he was a teacher and
worked in a bank and
later he helped run a
publishing company.
He was the first major
poet to write and
publish free verse in
England. At times it
is funny and rude.
Other times it is
deeply religious. Eliot
also wrote about
poetry, literature and
culture.*

Journey of the Magi

"A cold coming we had of it,
Just the worst time of the year
For a journey, and such a long journey:
The ways deep and the weather sharp,
The very dead of winter."
And the camels galled, sore-footed, refractory,
Lying down in the melting snow.
There were times we regretted
The summer palaces on slopes, the terraces,
And the silken girls bringing sherbet.
Then the camel men cursing and grumbling
And running away, and wanting their liquor and women,
And the night-fires going out, and the lack of shelters,
And the cities hostile and the towns unfriendly
And the villages dirty and charging high prices:
A hard time we had of it.
At the end we preferred to travel all night,
Sleeping in snatches,
With the voices singing in our ears, saying
That this was all folly.
Then at dawn we came down to a temperate valley,
Wet, below the snow line, smelling of vegetation;
With a running stream and a water-mill beating the darkness,
And three trees on the low sky.
And an old white horse galloped away in the meadow.
Then we came to a tavern with vine-leaves over the lintel,

Six hands at an open door dicing for pieces of silver,
And feet kicking the empty wine-skins.
But there was no information, and so we continued
And arrived at evening, not a moment too soon
Finding the place; it was (you may say) satisfactory.

All this was a long time ago, I remember,
And I would do it again, but set down
This set down
This: were we led all that way for
Birth or Death? There was a Birth, certainly,
We had evidence and no doubt. I had seen birth and death,
But had thought they were different; this Birth was
Hard and bitter agony for us, like Death, our death.
We returned to our places, these Kingdoms,
But no longer at ease here, in the old dispensation,
With an alien people clutching their gods.
I should be glad of another death. ◆

EDNA
ST VINCENT
MILLAY

1892–1950

Edna St Vincent
Millay was born in
Maine, USA. She
caused a huge stir
when her first book
of poems appeared,
because in certain
poems she portrayed
herself as reckless,
wild and fancy-free.
Some people welcomed
this as the arrival
of the new modern
woman in poetry,
but others thought it
was "naughty" and
outrageous.

The Fawn

There it was I saw what I shall never forget
And never retrieve.
Monstrous and beautiful to human eyes, hard to believe,
He lay, yet there he lay,
Asleep on the moss, his head on his polished cleft small
    ebony hooves,
The child of the doe, the dappled child of the deer.

Surely his mother had never said, "Lie here
Till I return," so spotty and plain to see
On the green moss lay he.
His eyes had opened; he considered me.

I would have given more than I care to say
To thrifty ears, might I have had him for my friend
One moment only of that forest day:

Might I have had the acceptance, not the love
Of those clear eyes;
Might I have been for him the bough above
Or the root beneath his forest bed,
A part of the forest, seen without surprise.

Was it alarm, or was it the wind of my fear lest he depart
That jerked him to his jointy knees,
And sent him crashing off, leaping and stumbling
On his new legs, between the stems of the white trees? ◆

Travel

The railroad track is miles away,
    And the day is loud with voices speaking,
Yet there isn't a train goes by all day
    But I hear its whistle shrieking.

All night there isn't a train goes by,
    Though the night is still for sleep and dreaming,
But I see its cinders red on the sky,
    And hear its engine steaming.

My heart is warm with the friends I make,
    And better friends I'll not be knowing;
Yet there isn't a train I wouldn't take,
    No matter where it's going. ◆

Dream Variations

To fling my arms wide,
In some place of the sun,
To whirl and to dance
Till the white day is done,
Then rest at cool evening
Beneath a tall tree
While night comes on gently,
    Dark like me, –
That is my dream!

To fling my arms wide,
In the face of the sun,
Dance! whirl! whirl!
Till the quick day is done,
Rest at pale evening…
A tall, slim tree…
Night coming tenderly,
    Black like me. ◆

LANGSTON
HUGHES

1902-1967

*Langston Hughes
is one of the most
famous African-
American writers of all
time. He was born in
Missouri, and he is
famous for being one
of the leaders of an
exciting explosion of
art, music and literature
known as the Harlem
Renaissance, in
New York. He made
his poems sound
like the speech and
songs of African-
Americans.*

Mother to Son

Well, son, I'll tell you:
Life for me ain't been no crystal stair.
It's had tacks in it,
And splinters,
And boards torn up,
And places with no carpet on the floor –
Bare.
But all the time
I's been a-climbin' on,
And reachin' landins,
And turnin' corners,
And sometimes goin' in the dark
Where there ain't been no light.
So boy, don't you turn back.
Don't you set down on the steps
'Cause you finds it's kinder hard.
Don't you fall now –
For I's still goin', honey,
I's still climbin',
And life for me ain't been no crystal stair. ◆

Final Curve

When you turn the corner
And you run into *yourself*
Then you know that you have turned
All the corners that are left. ◆

JUDITH
WRIGHT

1915-

*Judith Wright comes
from New South
Wales, and is one of
Australia's most famous
poets. She grew up on
her family's farm and
was educated at home
by Correspondence
School before going
away to school and then
to university in Sydney.
She has spent a great
deal of her time cam-
paigning for the rights
of the Aboriginal
peoples of Australia
and fighting against
the destruction of the
environment.*

Full Moon Rhyme

There's a hare in the moon tonight,
crouching alone in the bright
buttercup field of the moon;
and all the dogs in the world
howl at the hare in the moon.

"I chased that hare to the sky,"
the hungry dogs all cry.
"The hare jumped into the moon
and left me here in the cold.
I chased that hare to the moon."

"Come down again, wild hare.
We can see you there,"
the dogs all howl to the moon.
"Come down again to the world,
you mad black hare in the moon,

"or we will grow wings and fly
up to the star-grassed sky
to hunt you out of the moon,"
the hungry dogs of the world
howl at the hare in the moon. ◆

NOTES ON POEMS

Jacques ❖ 12

In the play, *As You Like It*, a duke has been dethroned and is living in exile in the Forest of Arden with a group of his court companions. One of these is Jacques, a fashionable young man often described as "affected" or what is nowadays sometimes called a "poser". The main character in the play, Rosalind, mocks him for this.

Caliban ❖ 14

Caliban is a character from *The Tempest*. He is a native of the island where the magical duke Prospero is shipwrecked with his daughter, Miranda. Prospero comes to rule over the island, and all its creatures and makes Caliban his servant.

At times, Caliban speaks very powerfully against Prospero saying, "This island's mine...", as he feels he has lost his freedom. Later in the play, he makes the mistake of thinking that two drunken sailors are going to help him fight back against Prospero.

Macbeth ❖ 15

Macbeth begins the play named after him as a successful soldier, but on his way home from battle he meets three witches who tell him that one day he will be King. He and his wife, Lady Macbeth, then plot how they will murder the present king. They kill the king and this crime leads them on to murdering others in the court. This speech comes at a time in the play when Macbeth is increasingly troubled by despair and guilt at what he has done.

Kubla Khan ❖ 24

Coleridge himself wrote about how he came to compose this poem. He said he fell asleep after reading an old travel book about the pleasure gardens in Xanadu that were built by the Mongol King of China, Khan Kublai, in the thirteenth century. In his sleep he dreamt the first fifty or so lines of a poem, and the moment he woke up hurried to write them down. But he never finished because he was interrupted by the arrival of a "person from Porlock", someone visiting him on business from a nearby town.

That's Coleridge's story, but some scholars think there are things wrong with it. For a start, the poem seems to be finished and not "interrupted". And the words of much of it are very similar to the old travel book – so similar that he could just have sat in his study rewriting the old book. And Coleridge has left out of the story one important fact that we know about him: he was a drug addict. Perhaps when he said he was asleep, he was hiding the fact that he was in a drugged state of mind.

The Destruction of Sennacherib ❖ 27

This tells the story of how King Sennacherib and his army were destroyed by the "Angel of Death". It's a Jewish story told in the Torah and the Old Testament of the Bible. Sennacherib was the King of Assyria (now Syria) in the eighth century BC. As Byron tells us in the poem, "the Assyrian" (which means the king and his army) attacked the land of Judah which is now part of Israel. "Deep Galilee" is the Sea of Galilee. The king's army, or as Byron says, "that host", were then killed by the "Angel of Death". This Angel is not like the pictures of angels that you see in most paintings and in churches. He is a terrifying servant of God who has it in his power to kill people and, so the story goes, on this occasion, destroyed more than a hundred and fifty thousand soldiers in King Sennacherib's army. The last verse of the poem talks of Ashur (a place in Assyria) and Baal, who is the idol that the people of Assyria were said to worship. The word "Gentile" is used to mean anyone who is not Jewish, and "the Lord" is, of course, the Jewish God.

La Belle Dame Sans Merci ❖ 32

This title is in French and means "The beautiful lady without pity". The poem is a "ballad" (see page 157). When Keats wrote *La Belle Dame Sans Merci*, it was becoming fashionable to take an interest in medieval matters – knights in armour, old ruined castles and churches. The results of this interest – known as the "Gothic" movement – can be found in many nineteenth-century buildings, and in poetry like this.

Paul Revere ❖ 46

Paul Revere (1735–1818) was a real historical figure. He was born in Boston, Massachusetts, and worked as a gold- and silversmith. Before the

"Ride" of the poem, Paul Revere was quite well-known as he had taken part in some of the first events of the American War of Independence. This was fought against the British (1775–1781). The poem is first and foremost a celebration of his midnight ride from Lexington to Concord to warn the people of the approach of British troops, but it is also, of course, a triumphant reminder of how Americans won their independence.

Eldorado or El Dorado ❖ 53

This is the name given to a legendary city or region believed to exist somewhere in the interior of South America. The story of Eldorado, a vast city of gold that lay on golden sands by a great inland lake, came from Spanish soldiers exploring the River Orinoco in the sixteenth century. Many expeditions set out to look for Eldorado but it was never found.

My Last Duchess ❖ 66

When we read this poem we have to imagine that it is a kind of speech, being made by a duke – the husband of a duchess who has died. Her picture has been painted by Fra Pandolf. The duke asks a group of visitors to look at it. We discover bit by bit what has been going on before this moment: the duke was angry because his wife, according to him, was "too easily impressed". She did not seem to think her marriage to a duke (with hundreds of years of history to his name) any more important than, say, someone giving her a bunch of cherries. Then the duke says, "I gave commands; Then all smiles stopped together". Many people read that as meaning: I gave orders for her to be killed. In the last part of the poem, we gather that the visitors come from a count who is interested in his daughter marrying this duke. The duke makes it clear that he expects a great deal of money from the count if this happens: "your munificence/Is ample warrant that no just pretence/Of mine for dowry will be disallowed". This means: your well-known wealth is a good enough guarantee that I can ask for really big money when I marry the daughter and your master won't refuse it.

  My Last Duchess is a fine example of writing where the reader can work out many more things about the speaker than he or she is actually saying. This is called "irony".

Mannahatta ❖ 74

The word "Mannahatta" is a variation on Manhattan, the original native American name for the island on which New York is built. Whitman was the first American poet to write about city life and this is what he said about "Mannahatta":
"How fit a name for America's great democratic island city! The word itself, how beautiful! how it seems to rise with tall spires, glistening in sunshine, with New World atmosphere…"

O Captain! My Captain! ❖ 76

This poem was written as a way of mourning the death of the American president, Abraham Lincoln. Lincoln was the president who led the north against the south in the American Civil War, which was partly (but only partly!) a war about ending slavery. Lincoln became a hero for people who wanted all human beings to be equal and free, but he was assassinated – shot when he was at the theatre. A poem written to mourn someone's death is called an "elegy".

How Doth The Little Crocodile ❖ 87

This is a "parody" – a poem that takes the shape and sound of an existing poem and puts new words to it (see page 157). Here is the poem Lewis Carroll used:

Against Idleness and Mischief

How doth the little busy bee
Improve each shining hour
And gather honey all the day,
From every opening flower!

How skilfully she builds her cell!
How neat she spreads her wax!
And labours hard to store it well
With the sweet food she makes.

In works of labour, or of skill,
I would be busy too;
For Satan finds some mischief still
For idle hands to do.

In books, or work, or healthful play,
Let my first years be past;
That I may give for every day
Some good account at last.

Written by Isaac Watts and published in 1715, this became one of the most well-known poems in the English language, as children were taught to recite it over and over again in schools and Sunday schools. As you can see, it is a kind of prayer to encourage children to do something useful every day. Carroll's crocodile seems to have found another way to "improve" himself!

Iroquois Prayer ❖ 90
The Iroquois were the Native Americans who lived around the lower Great Lakes in upper New York state. The five Iroquois nations were the Mohawk, Oneida, Onandaga, Cayuga and Seneca. They formed the "Iroquois League" sometime between 1570 and 1600. This prayer of thanks comes from one of the agricultural festivals that the Iroquois nations celebrated.

Waltzing Matilda ❖ 104
Here are explanations of some of the Australian words in this poem:

> swagman – *a travelling bush-worker;*
> billabong – *a pool left behind when a river changes course;*
> billy – *a little can or pot that you can put on a fire to cook with;*
> jumbuck – *a kind of sheep;*
> tucker bag – *a food bag;*
> squatter – *a well-off landowner, usually English in origin;*
> thoroughbred – *a very good pure-bred horse;*
> troopers – *mounted police.*

A Smuggler's Song ❖ 110
The kind of smuggling written about in this poem is what some country people used to do in the eighteenth and nineteenth centuries to avoid paying the government taxes on such things as brandy, lace and tobacco being shipped to Britain from France. If you were caught, you could be hanged or sent to Australia as a convict. The Parson is the local vicar, the Clerk is someone who works for a lawyer, and "King George's men" are soldiers. Trusty and Pincher are dogs. A cap of Valenciennes is a cap made of lace.

The Deep-sea Cables ❖ 112
One of the greatest wonders of the new technological age of the nineteenth century was the telephone. And the greatest wonder of the telephone was that it made it possible to talk to someone on the other side of the world. This first happened when deep-sea cables were laid on the floor of the Atlantic Ocean in 1866.

Tarantella ❖ 122
This poem talks of someone who remembers an occasion at an inn in the "High Pyrenees", the mountains that run between France and Spain. A "tarantella" is a kind of dance that people were doing at the inn. Originally the tarantella came from Italy and is in 6/8 time. The poem captures the rhythm of the dance.

Journey of the Magi ❖ 144
This is a "dramatic monologue" (see page 157) put into the mouth of one of the "Three Wise Men" or "The Three Kings". These were the men who appear in the New Testament following a star to the stable in Nazareth where Jesus Christ has just been born. They bring gifts of frankincense, myrrh and gold. The word "Magi" is a Latin word meaning "wise and magical men", "sages" or "shamans".

Notes about poetry

Sonnet
This is a poem that is fourteen lines long and usually rhymes. It was a way of writing that first appeared in Italy and was brought into English writing in the sixteenth century. At that time, sonnets had two parts: the first was eight lines long, then there was a kind of pause – or change of thought – before the last six lines. Some of the most famous writers of sonnets were Shakespeare, Donne, Milton, Wordsworth, Elizabeth Barrett Browning and Keats.

Dramatic Monologue
This is a poem that is written in the voice of someone talking about a scene that he or she is taking part in. Quite often the person who is speaking talks to someone else in the scene. In other words, the poem is like a speech out of a play or a film. The long speeches by the characters in Shakespeare's plays are called "soliloquies" but they are, in a way, dramatic monologues. Robert Browning was one of the first people to write dramatic monologues as poems, but other poets who've written them include Tennyson, Hardy, Kipling, Robert Frost and T. S. Eliot.

Free Verse
This is a way of describing poems that do not rhyme and do not have a regular rhythm. Walt Whitman (page 72) was one of the first poets to publish free verse poetry. However, the first people to translate the Old Testament into English in the sixteenth century were really turning Hebrew songs like "The Song of Solomon" into free verse poems. In France, in the nineteenth century, some poets started to experiment writing very short poetic paragraphs that people have called "prose poems". Between 1890 and 1920, quite a few poets in France, Belgium, America and England wrote free verse, including Carl Sandburg and T. S. Eliot.

Ballad
This is a way of writing a story in verses. These verses are four lines long and rhyme on the second and fourth lines. They are called "quatrains" and usually have four beats for the first and third lines and three beats for the second and fourth. The first ballads were anonymous – that is to say no one knew exactly who made them up. In Elizabethan times people started selling ballads on the street, at fairs and in taverns, rather like people sell newspapers today. These were written by poets whose names have disappeared, but later, from about 1700 onwards, more famous poets like Keats enjoyed writing ballads.

Lyric
This is a word used to describe any short poem that expresses a poet's personal feelings and thoughts. These can be about love or about a person, a place, a memory or something that the poet hopes will happen. In this book, Thomas Hardy's *At the Railway Station, Upway*, and Langston Hughes's *Dream Variations* are lyrics. Sometimes the word "lyric" is also used in a different way to mean "the words of a song", as in "Bernie Taupin writes the lyrics of Elton John's songs".

Parody
A parody is a special way of copying or mimicking someone else's writing style. In poetry, the poet often takes the shape of the original poem and changes some or most of the words. Sometimes this is done to mock the original poet's way of writing, but at other times it's just a way of having fun. In a Punch and Judy show, Punch will parody Shakespeare's line "To be or not to be, that is the question" by saying to his dog, "Toby or not Toby, that is the question". Lewis Carroll was very fond of parodies (see pages 87 and 155).

Blank Verse
This is poetry that doesn't rhyme but has a regular rhythm, the "iambic pentameter". "Pentameter" means that each line has five strong beats and "iambic" means that each strong beat has an offbeat just before it, like this: te-TUM, te-TUM, te-TUM, te-TUM, te-TUM. One "te-TUM" is called an "iamb". The first writers to use blank verse in England were in Elizabethan times. Most of Shakespeare's plays are written in blank verse.
Here's a regular blank verse line from "Macbeth":

And **All** our **Yes**ter**Days** have **Light**ed **Fools**

te **Tum** te **Tum** te**Tum** te **Tum** te **Tum**

Part of the trick of writing interesting blank verse is to write it so that it is not always absolutely regular "te-TUM, te-TUM".

INDEX OF TITLES AND FIRST LINES

ACKNOWLEDGEMENTS

"The Wind begun to knead the Grass –", "A slash of Blue –", "A Bird came down the Walk –", "A word is dead", "I'm Nobody! Who are you?" by Emily Dickinson, reprinted by permission of the publishers and the Trustees of Amherst College from *The Poems of Emily Dickinson*, Thomas H. Johnson, ed., Cambridge, Mass., USA. The Belknap Press of Harvard University Press, Copyright © 1951, 1955, 1979, 1983 by the President and Fellows of Harvard College.

Snow in the Suburbs, Throwing a Tree and *At the Railway Station, Upway* by Thomas Hardy, from *The Complete Poems*, reprinted by permission of Papermac.

Waltzing Matilda and *Mulga Bill's Bicycle* by A.B. Paterson from his COLLECTED POEMS, © 1921 Retusa Pty Limited.

A Smuggler's Song from *Puck of Pook's Hill* and *The Way Through the Woods* from *Rewards and Fairies*, both by Rudyard Kipling, reprinted by permission of A P Watt Ltd on behalf of The National Trust for Places of Historic Interest or Natural Beauty.

The Song of Wandering Aengus, The Lake Isle of Innisfree, He Wishes For the Cloths of Heaven and *An Irish Airman Foresees His Death*, from *The Collected Poems of W B Yeats*, reprinted by permission of A P Watt Ltd on behalf of Michael Yeats.

Tarantella by Hilaire Belloc from *Complete Verse* published by Pimlico, reprinted by permission of the Estate of Hilaire Belloc and Peters Fraser & Dunlop Group Ltd.

The Listeners, Silver and *Five Eyes* by Walter de la Mare, reprinted by permission of The Literary Trustees of Walter de la Mare, and the Society of Authors as their representative.

Stopping by Woods on a Snowy Evening, The Pasture and *The Road Not Taken* from *The Poetry of Robert Frost* edited by Edward Connery Lathem. Copyright © 1951 by Robert Frost. Reprinted by permission of Jonathan Cape Ltd.

Arithmetic and *Skyscraper* from The Complete Poems of Carl Sandburg, copyright © 1950 by Carl Sandburg and renewed 1978 by Margaret Sandburg, Helga Sandburg Crile, and Janet Sandburg, reprinted by permission of Harcourt Brace & Company.

Cargoes by John Masefield, reprinted by permission of The Society of Authors as the literary representative of the Estate of John Masefield.

The General by Siegfried Sassoon, reprinted by permission of George Sassoon.

Journey of the Magi by T. S. Eliot, from *Collected Poems 1909-1962*, reprinted by permission of Faber & Faber Ltd.

Travel and *The Fawn* by Edna St Vincent Millay, from *Collected Poems*, published by Harper Collins. Copyright © 1921, 1934, 1948 and 1962 by Edna St Vincent Millay and Norma Millay Ellis. Reprinted by permission of Elizabeth Barnett, literary executor.

Mother to Son, Final Curve, Dream Variations from *Selected Poems by Langston Hughes*, copyright © 1994 the Estate of Langston Hughes, reprinted by permission of Harold Ober Associates, Inc.

Full Moon Rhyme by Judith Wright, from *Collected Poems*, reprinted by permission of Harper Collins Publishers.

While every effort has been made to obtain permission, in some cases it has been difficult to trace the copyright holders, and we would like to apologize for any apparent negligence.